Creative Strategic Planning—An Oxymoron

Creative Strategic Planning—An Oxymoron

A unique, creative, non linear approach to strategy development

Dennis C. Leslie

Phoenix Consulting

To order additional copies of this book, contact:
Xlibris Corporation
1-888-795-4274
www.Xlibris.com
Orders@Xlibris.com
20762

CONTENTS

Preliminary Comments

The approach and concepts I cover in this book, though not based upon a scientific research study from an academic institution or a large consulting company, are based upon a lot of data points from over fourteen years as a consultant spent on assisting hundreds of organizations in developing breakthrough strategies. I gleaned information not only from the companies but also from the thousands of managers that participated in these strategy development efforts.

Strategy development is a confidential matter for most organizations. I have utilized examples that are both true and representative of the types of real live strategies that evolve out of the processes and tools I cover. However, the names and specifics of the situation have been altered to honor the confidentiality of my work with them. All of my engagements come from references and referrals. Clients are more than happy to share their experiences individually with other companies but are naturally reluctant to broadcast their experiences to the whole world.

Some feel that it is some sort of management failure to need the help of an outsider. Nothing can be further from the truth. A fresh set of eyes, processes, and tools can be very useful in breaking out of our own paradigms. Others do not want to show some of their own fallibilities that they discovered and addressed. Some have strategies still in force today, and they wish to keep them under the radar of their competitors. For all of these reasons, I choose to keep their identities unrevealed.

My teaching of strategy development and implementation in the graduate school of business of the University of St. Thomas in Minneapolis, Minnesota, over the last twelve years has provided another set of data points. Having taught over thirty-six courses in the Executive MBA program gave me additional exposure to hundreds of other companies beyond my consulting practice and to many different levels within organizations. I saw how strategy development changed over the years with changes in management and perspectives at all sized companies including divisions of multinational firms. The teaching experience added another seven hundred-plus individual managers to my resource of observations.

Lastly, I have drawn strategy development experiences from my sixteen years of working for a variety of companies in marketing management, sales management, and general management positions.

The processes and tools I cover are not hard and fast absolute rules that must be slavishly followed, but a series of guidelines that have been developed over the years and have successfully stood the test of time. They have been applied to not-for-profit and for-profit organizations, large and small public companies, and private companies as well. Though most effective at the company level, the approach I outline is also quite useful at the department level and even at a project level.

Acknowledgements

I do not believe I could have completed this book without the continuous help and support of my long-term business associate, Colleen Simcoe. She tirelessly assisted me in all phases of the book, and, as always, kept me on the straight and narrow path.

The knowledge I share are based upon my experiences with all of my past employers, clients, the students I have taught at the University of St. Thomas, and the faculty of the business school. They all have provided the grist for my observations and approaches, and I thank them all.

Last but not the least, I thank my wife, Lori, along with all of my friends and colleagues, for putting up with all of my foibles and idiosyncrasies throughout my business career.

The Opening Gambit to Creative Strategic Planning . . . An Oxymoron

It seems managers spend about 95 percent of their day stomping out current fires or seizing quick opportunities in today's fast-paced business world. These managers, though excellent firefighters, may actually be arsonists without realizing it! A quick solution to a problem's symptoms or only a piece of the problem leaves the major underlying issues or root causes unaddressed, creating more fires down the road. The quick fix or Band-Aid approach rarely lasts very long. The Band-Aid eventually falls off, and the wound grows worse. Repeat this often enough, and irreparable damage may be done.

Even worse, many businesses fall into a sorry state of trying to reduce costs in an effort to attain improved profitability. These organizations are simply "doing last year harder" in the hope that the old way of doing things will somehow miraculously work again.

In many ways, business has lost its ability to creatively develop new ways to reach more customers through new products and services, as well as developing innovative ways to please customers.

The Fallacies of Creative Strategy

It's no wonder: A few of us have received formal education on how to be creative, nor does much useful information exist on how to develop creativity in an organizational setting.

Don't get me wrong. A plethora of books, business articles, and consultants abound, all touting that they have the best strategies to develop creativity. It doesn't matter whether it is Porter's Five Forces, Boston Consulting Group's Growth-Share Matrix, or McKinsey & Co.'s Seven S's Model. A broad and endless menu is available for anyone to choose from.

But do you really know if this hot selection-of-the-month strategy will fit your organization and your specific situation? That it will actually work? What happens if your largest competitor is reading the same books and selecting the same strategies?

Another fallacy about creating strategy is that the folks at the top of the organization should do it. The reality is, these are the people who have been the most removed from the actual firing line of the marketplace for years. They have a vested interest in defending and maintaining current strategies that may have led them to their current position. I also believe that one's ability to think innovatively about the marketplace is often inversely related to one's level in the organizational hierarchy.

Some management teams have worked together so long that they are guilty of groupthink and don't even know it. Why not involve and search out ideas from all areas and levels of the organization rather than just rely on the top managers and their direct reports?

While we're at it, why don't we let go of the obsessive slavery to the numbers? Focusing on numbers never leads to creative strategy. Instead, it leads to backing into the numbers and only incremental change. It also forestalls true strategic discussion with excuses such as "it is not in the budget or it will not pay for itself within eighteen months." The reality is, most significant new strategies don't fit into the annual budget nor can they pay back their costs quickly enough to please the accountants and finance experts.

Virtually all of the tools for evaluating a potential strategy are financial in nature and involve forecasts, no matter whether it's a return on invested capital, a break-even analysis, or an economic value-added analysis. A forecast is simply an educated guess and nothing more. Most companies cannot accurately forecast where they will finish the year, let alone forecast the impact of a creative new strategy three years out.

The quickest way to strangle the life out of any incipient creative strategy before it has time to grow and develop into something truly innovative and meaningful is to run the numbers on it. Strategy drives the numbers, not the reverse. Why not take the time to explore why a creative strategy can work and the benefit derived from it before we evaluate it?

> ## Strategy Drives the Numbers Not the Reverse

Breaking the Rules

In order to be truly innovative, we must remove the structured processes that stand in the way of creativity. We must hold at bay the many business tools and evaluation techniques. We must seek out new information and new perspectives beyond just picking from a preordained set of strategies existing in the business literature.

Lest I leave you with the wrong impression, I am not saying that a lot of the business tools and concepts that exist in books and business literature are bad. On the contrary, they can be quite useful. You just need to recognize their inherent weaknesses and limitations. They should be used only as techniques to initiate the discussion, not limit it. They should be used to help get the ball rolling towards creativity and innovation. Because in essence, we must discover our own path!

It is interesting to note that most of the truly creative innovations to hit an industry come from outside of it. For example, shouldn't UPS or the U.S. Postal Service have developed the overnight delivery of documents and small packages instead of the upstart Federal Express? Shouldn't word processor companies such as Wang or CPT have come up with the personal computer rather than the upstart Apple? Why does this happen? New entrants do not follow the rules of the industry or the conventional wisdom. They create their own rules for success that often turn an industry on its ear. Creative strategy is about breaking the rules. Not just the industry rules but also your own internal rules, or mental models that hold you back.

Imagine what it must have been like when the U.S. Forest Service discovered that the best way to extinguish a large uncontrolled forest fire was to create a backfire in front of it starving the fire of fuel so it goes out all on its own. I would bet that the first firefighter to suggest this possibility was met with a good deal of disbelief. Go back to biblical times and the story of David and Goliath. David didn't offer to fight the giant hand to hand or to arm wrestle him. He stood off in the distance with a sling and nailed Goliath with a rock to win the battle. So change your path, create your own rules and your new future.

Chapter 1

Why Bother?

Over the last decade, there have been dozens of articles and books published, either praising the benefits and need for strategic planning, or professing that it is an arcane tool that is no longer relevant in a fast-changing world environment. You can take your pick as which to believe. However, surveys conducted by major associations show that approximately half of the *Fortune* 1000 companies did no strategic planning at all. Worse yet, over 75 percent of those that did it were not happy with their process. With this conflicting literature, it is no wonder that effective strategic planning is in such a sorry state.

The term "strategic planning" is truly an oxymoron. The word "strategic" generates thoughts of creativity, innovation, and something that is truly different. Yet, the word "planning" suggests careful analysis with lots of process, steps and forms that are the antithesis of creativity! Is it possible to combine both concepts into something worthwhile? The answer is a resounding yes, but it cannot be achieved in the traditional linear manner that is common in management today. This book will outline a different approach to strategic planning that uses many of the fine business concepts that are already proven successful but connects them in a very different fashion. It also debunks some very ingrained processes and misuse of business concepts in the search for that illusive beast called effective strategy.

The approach I cover is an open-ended overall architecture. It is designed to make you think through your processes and tools so that structure does not throttle your organization's creativity. I am not suggesting that you replace one restrictive structure for strategic planning with another restrictive one. It is a framework to help you use your creative strategy development structure as an enabler of creativity rather than a constraint. The book is not intended to provide a detailed road map but directional principles.

To help make the shift in thinking from planning to strategy, I will replace the term strategic planning with the term strategy development. In the old style of strategic planning, it seemed that 90 percent of the effort was placed on the planning portion such as filling out all the myriad forms required by very structured processes. Only 10 percent of the time was spent on developing truly innovative strategies. In strategy development, we reverse these percentages and devote most of our time and energy to creative strategy development, which is the difficult, yet fun part of the process. Once we are done with the creative effort, then we fit it into any format we desire.

TIME AND EFFORT SPENT		
	STRATEGY	*PLANNING*
OLD MODEL	10%	90%
NEW APPROACH	90%	10%

Before we begin the journey, we must ask why we are making such a trip in the first place. As with many management concepts, businesses often embark on a strategy development effort with no real sense of the expected outcome of the project. There are a ton of secondary reasons for strategy development. These reasons may include:

- The board of directors wants one
- We have always done one
- Everybody is doing it
- The banks want to see one
- We need it to raise more capital
- A recent write-up in a business magazine
- We need an exit plan to help sell the business

If there is one fundamental you must accept to succeed in effective strategy development it is this: The only reason to undertake a strategy development effort is to dramatically improve the measurable results of the organization. We are not talking about just tweaking performance . . . that is for annual business planning. Effective strategy development requires too much time, effort, and agonizing choices to undertake for just incremental gain. It is a roadmap to fundamentally change the way you run the organization. The task at hand is not for the weak of heart! The long-term success of the organization is at stake.

> **The only reason to undertake a strategy development effort is to dramatically improve the measurable results of the organization.**

Chapter 2

What It Ain't

This fundamental objective of significantly improving results by changing the way you run the organization is at odds with prevailing views of the purpose of strategy development. It may be appropriate to list the current activities that masquerade as strategy development.

Strategy Development is Not Five-Year Planning

There is no set time framework for strategy development. Five years is several lifetimes for a high-tech company where new technologies emerge and markets evaporate in the blink of a quarter. However, five years is a very short time for a utility where it takes more than five years to build a new power plant. The planning horizon will be different for different industries and different companies in those industries. A new significant strategy may change an organization's direction and results quickly while others will take time to grab hold and pay off. The strategies developed actually determine the proper time frame for the plan.

Strategy Development is Not Projections

Most organizations cannot accurately forecast the current year's final numbers when they are in the tenth month, let alone forecast three or five years out. Give it up! At worst, such forecasts are a fiction, and at best, they are an educated guess. Too many plans are merely an effort to back into some predetermined forecast. Often, a multiplier is applied to the current year's numbers. This is so common that it has an acronym, CAGR, which stands for Corporate Annual Growth Rate. Use any multiplier you want . . . it has absolutely nothing to do with reality. Neither the past nor the present can be used to forecast the future. The past is past, the present is now, and the only thing we can accurately predict is that the future will be different! The warning sign that you are prey to this forecasting myth is when the organization will not begin its long-term planning until it finalizes this year's numbers. After all, you have to have a base for the multiplier! Worse yet, when planners from different divisions start comparing each other's CAGRs, now you really are in trouble. The second fundamental you need to accept is that projections are fiction, so give them up.

> Projections are fiction,
> so give them up.

Strategy Development Is Not A Two-Day Brainstorming Conference

Most two-day strategy development conferences are done with little or no preparation and are held off-site in a nice resort setting where some team building sport such as golf is readily available. The agenda is first set based on tee times, cocktails, and the obligatory dinners. Outside speakers may be brought in not only to augment the organization's own top brass's speeches but also to help fill the allotted planning time. Group discussions fill out the rest of the time required to prove to the IRS that the boondoggle truly was a strategy development conference. Since no preparation was done, the discussions eventually distill down to the decision that the organization should just do last year harder. Time gets short so everyone vows to work with more enthusiasm and commitment next year. The conference is proclaimed a success since everyone accepts that the real value is the team building that goes on during golf and drinks. Participants leave happy, the flip-chart sheets are misplaced and in three weeks' time, all is forgotten until the next session.

Effective strategy development is not complicated, but it does take time and preparation which is why it is so often avoided or done superficially.

Strategy Development Is Not Annual Business Planning

Annual business planning is important and it is a last step in the strategy development process but it is not the process itself. Annual business planning by its nature has some very significant drawbacks that limit one's ability to think creatively and for the long term. First, since it is annual, it only looks out twelve months. It is difficult to address those possibilities that span more than one year since oftentimes, strategic initiatives cannot be accomplished in just one year. In addition, the budgeting and financial ramifications of a new long-term strategy may well exceed the twelve-month period. Departments as part of their budgeting processes often construct annual plans. As a result, those tough issues which usually cross over departmental boundaries are not dealt with. Annual plans tend to consider those efforts that can be done in twelve months, addressed within one department, and fall within the twelve-month budget cycle.

Strategy Development Is Not Just The Domain Of The Top Managers Of The Organization

It is difficult to avoid groupthink if only the top three or four people are involved in strategy development. You need to cast the net very wide in order to capture the diversity of thought and experience that is available to you through the variety of people employed in the organization. Anyone, anywhere in the organization may come up with that breakthrough strategy if you encourage his or her input and participation in the process. Moreover, you will gain the added advantage of their commitment to carrying out the final plan because they had a hand in its development.

All participants must keep in mind that such involvement is participative management; it is not a democracy. Top management is ultimately responsible for developing the strategies, executing them, and obtaining the anticipated results.

Chapter 3

What Drives People to Do It?

Folks go through the effort to plan creatively and strategically because the world around us is changing fast.

Markets And Products Change

Markets emerge, grow, mature, and evaporate at an unprecedented rate. So many new technologies are on the horizon; it is very difficult to determine which ones will become commercially successful and which will fade faster than the setting sun at dusk.

Competitors Change

The competitive landscape changes daily. It is not enough to keep abreast of the traditional competitors who look and act like us. Well-established companies with deep pockets are looking to grow in new markets . . . yours! Your worst nightmare is the new emerging competitor that is not even on your radar screen. They do not have to follow the industry norms because they are new to it and may not even know them. They tend to come up with the truly innovative value propositions. Moreover, they can sneak up on you. They could be your customers, your vendors, or even your own employees.

Employees Change

The changing values of people are not just changing customer expectations but also employee expectations. There is no more implied employment contract between employer and employee anymore. It is becoming harder to attract and retain good talent. Employees are no longer willing to wait long for promotions or expansion of their jobs. They are also less willing to relocate and to work fifty to sixty-plus hours a week. They want and expect to have a life away from work.

Rules Change

The myriad of governmental regulations continues to change and grow at an unprecedented rate.

Managers Plan Strategically Out Of Anxiety, Frustration, Or Desperation

With all of the aforementioned change, and without a guiding strategic plan, you may feel caught between the proverbial rock and a hard place. This sea of change creates one of the essential three emotions (anxiety, frustration, or desperation) that drive you to undertake the organization's first strategy plan or to consider a very serious and thorough review of the current plan.

Pro-active managers or organizations develop strategy out of **anxiety**. They are already doing very well and have done so for many quarters or several years. Owners, stockholders, and employees have come to expect continued high levels of success. Even a minor slip in a public corporation's quarterly earnings can quickly trash the stock price. Employees have been taking raises and bonuses for granted. A slowdown, however well warranted, is very unnerving to them. In effect, the organization has become a victim of its own success and the pressure is on to maintain past glory.

Yet, remaining successful, whether success is measured in volume or profit growth, becomes more difficult the larger you become. You are now a bigger target on your competitors' radar screens. It takes a lot more effort just to maintain the present level of activity, let alone grow it. A pro-active company needs to chart new avenues of growth while maintaining the success of current endeavors. This challenge drives the fear and the necessity to develop new strategies.

The second emotion that sets a strategy development effort in motion is the **frustration** that a marginally performing company endures. By marginal performance, I mean organizations that are not experiencing their traditional level of success. They may be nicely profitable or growing but not at the desired rate. Perhaps they are not matching the growth rates of the industry or no longer getting the high stock valuations they once enjoyed. Usually, this situation has been going on for sometime. Most organizations and their managers are masters of rationalization. The first bad year was a fluke, then maybe it was a weakening of the economy and then it was a softening of the industry. Eventually, just like an alcoholic that hits bottom before seeking help, the managers look in the mirror and realize that maybe they had something to do with the poor results. Now it is time to figure out a different program.

Finally, for those companies or organizations that strategize out of **desperation**, I refer to them as pre-chapter 11 organizations. If they do not get off the dime quick, they will not be around next quarter. Such organizations have doctorate degrees in rationalization. They have been to the brink of extinction several times before and have somehow managed to pull a rabbit out of the hat. They truly believe that they can do it repeatedly. The need for a different direction is often forced upon them by the external world when a key vendor cuts them off, the bank tightens down on the line of credit, or they lose vital employees. Their task is to develop a comprehensive strategy plan that will help them survive not only in the long term but also in the next quarter!

Chapter 4

When to Develop New Strategies

The best time to undertake your first strategy development effort or to update your current one is right now. You often hear managers say they are too busy with present work to do any real strategy development. The fallacy here is that an organization is constantly making large strategic decisions but without the benefit of an overall framework. A framework tests whether actions make sense long-term and if strategies actually work together or conflict with one another. A strategy plan provides this framework.

Another excuse is that we have already done the budgeting for this year and we should wait for the next budgeting cycle. In reality, most new strategies do not involve a lot of new budget dollars in the first year. Strategy development is a matter of shifting the focus of your energy to new programs that will pave the way for a more successful future. It is best to follow that old Bedouin saying that the time to dig a well is before you are thirsty!

Most planning efforts are instigated as a result of some external event. It may be the significant growth of a new or existing competitor, the emergence of a new technology, the loss of a large customer, new ownership of the company, or a new CEO that wants to make his or her mark. The time to strike is while the iron is hot. Some companies actually use an event to marshal peoples' enthusiasm for change.

The only individual who truly relishes change is a baby with dirty diapers. Without a focal point or event, employees and managers may not feel the need for change and will resist it because of all of the uncertainty it brings. One way that a small foundering country revitalizes a sense of national unity is by starting a war . . . nothing like a highly visible common enemy to pull people together! I have dubbed this phenomenon the Evil Empire Syndrome. It can be very effective. To get the process rolling, identify an event or compelling need for change, name it the Evil Empire and let the strategy development begin.

Chapter 5

The Basic Components of a
Strategic Plan

A lmost all strategic plans use similar components that are depicted in the strategy development pyramid. Companies may call each of the components different names but the basic hierarchy of relationships remains the same.

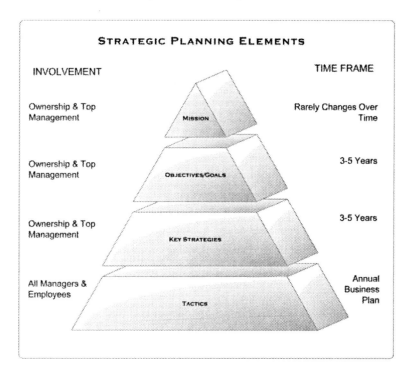

STRATEGIC PLANNING ELEMENTS

INVOLVEMENT		TIME FRAME
Ownership & Top Management	MISSION	Rarely Changes Over Time
Ownership & Top Management	OBJECTIVES/GOALS	3-5 Years
Ownership & Top Management	KEY STRATEGIES	3-5 Years
All Managers & Employees	TACTICS	Annual Business Plan

Mission

Simply put, a mission statement is the organization's thirty-second commercial to the world. It states who you are, what you do, who you do it for, and how you do it differently from anyone else. It should be short so that everyone in the company can remember it or easily restate it in their own words. It is often referred to as the elevator message, i.e., you can convey it in an elevator ride. It should use simple short words so anyone can comprehend it. It should be specific enough that it describes only your organization and could not be applied to your competitor. A quick way to determine if it is understood and effective is to randomly ask employees what the mission of the organization is and see how close they come to it.

Unfortunately, mission statements, all too often, are merely politically correct statements that are so general in nature they could apply to anyone in your industry. Often they are rarely looked at or communicated. Sometimes (gasp) they are even left to the communications department to create and are more of a marketing tool than a guide to the organization. They may be hidden away on a plaque somewhere in the bowels of the organization. Some companies, however, do an excellent job of discussing the mission and all of its ramifications with new employees.

The mission statement performs a dual role in guiding the organization. It not only tells you what business you are in, but more importantly, it also tells you the inverse by omission . . . what businesses you are not in! Too many companies plunge into totally new businesses without ever considering the true consequences. This statement is especially true in the case of acquisitions designed to fuel a company's growth. Just think of how many times you have read about a divestiture where the press release indicated that the acquisition did not meet the company's strategic focus. Translation: They did not know what their strategic focus was! Either they had no real mission statement or they did not follow it. Before attempting an acquisition, look to see if it really meets the mission. If not, think again. If the acquisition is still a go, then the mission should be changed to accommodate it. You have to strain the gray matter a bit to develop a mission that is not so narrow that you will quickly outgrow it, yet not so broad that you can do just about anything you wish.

Vision Statement

It proclaims who you want to be, where you are going, and what you are striving for. The vision statement is not an essential part of the strategy plan but can be an enhancement to it. Often, the feel of a vision actually shows up in the mission. Just do not confuse the vision with the mission.

Philosophy Or Guiding Principles Or Value Statements

These statements can be nice additions to a strategy plan as long as they are not substituted for a mission statement. Usually all three areas influence the organization. Explicitly stating them can be of real benefit if they reflect reality. However, it is common to have a large disconnect between what is stated and what actually happens. This situation is far more damaging to the morale of the employees than not having these types of statements at all. Employees see them as a written promise. So be careful, use them only if they are accurate.

Goals And Objectives

These components are critical to a successful strategy plan. A goal is the word statement depicting what you want to achieve. For example, you may want to be the industry leader. The objective is measurable and dated; it lets you know when you have reached the goal and can throw the party. For example, with the above goal, the objective may be to have sales volume larger than any of your main competitors or it could be any number of financial measures such as profitability or return on investment.

The objective does not have to be stated financially. For example, it could be stated as number of patients served or members added to an association. It should just be numeric in some way so it is definitive when it is reached. Again, this is one set of definitions; some organizations reverse the descriptions, some use different terms such as outcomes or milestones. Just make sure that everyone in your organization is using the same terminology and understands the definitions since they will be held accountable to them. To be effective, goals and objectives must be set realistically with enough stretch to drive significant improvement but not so high as to be dismissed by most as unattainable. In addition, setting the bar too low does nothing to improve performance, let alone lead to significant and lasting change.

Key Strategies

Key strategies are the backbone of a strategy plan. They are the drivers. Key strategies are the net new initiatives that will propel the organization forward. They include either new approaches that you will implement or old ones that you will abandon. They tend to take several years to implement, they cut across departments, and they impact the entire organization. Because of the resources they require, and the amount of change involved, they should be few in number (less than four or five and certainly no more than ten). There is a finite amount of change any organization can endure.

Remember that the Ten Commandments directed a lot of the Judeo-Christian world for thousands of years before the Bible was written. The Commandments are key strategies that have proven to be very effective and lasting. And just like the strategies of a solid strategy plan, they are not optional but mandatory! Eight out of ten is not acceptable no matter how much some of us would like it to be so. If strategies are considered or treated as optional, there is no plan. A menu of ideas that you can choose from only leads to a half-hearted, fragmented effort.

Tactics Or Action Items

Tactics or action items are the smaller steps taken in shorter periods by specific people to accomplish the strategies. These are actions that are planned for the next year and are often budgeted in the various departments. Tactics are the blocking and tackling of a strategy plan. They ensure that enough progress is made on the new strategies. All too often, we get wrapped around the axle just trying to keep the current business rolling. We never seem to have the time to work on big improvements. The tactics keep the strategies front and center by working them into the annual business plan. They help manage the creative tension that arises when you need to run the current business as effectively as you can, often called "managing the first curve," while simultaneously creating the new future, the second curve. Keep in mind that tactics may change over the course of the year based on the judgment of the person carrying them out. The strategy it is supporting, however, does not change unless the entire strategy team agrees. A change in strategy is usually due to unforeseen changes in the external environment.

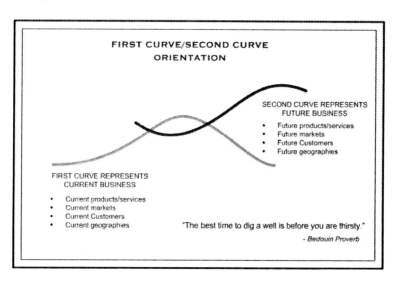

Chapter 6

The Basic Process for

Developing the Strategy Plan

M any books have been written on the components of a plan, dissecting them, showing lots of examples and some tools for getting at them, but none really address the overall process of putting together a powerful strategy plan. All you really need to remember are the Four D's of strategy development, **Data, Discussion, Decide and Do**.

Data

I estimate that over 70 percent of strategy development efforts fail because they are not based upon enough factual data. Organizations try to leap directly into strategy creation without the benefit of a thorough analysis of the current state of affairs. Members of the traditional planning team draw upon their own long-held perceptions of the world and what needs to be done, in effect, hardening their own positions rather than searching out new information that will open their thinking. A lack of real data is obvious when you see planning sessions degenerate into arguments about what the facts truly are. Worse yet, you enter a planning session with ten issues and come out with the original ten plus five more. A thorough analysis provides the data and perspective to springboard into the generation of truly innovative change.

Several basic rules apply to the collection of data:

1. Collect both internal data such as sales, costs, and profitability numbers and trends along with external data such as customer research, industry trends, and competition analysis.
2. Use multiple data sources and perspectives. Do not rely just on the sales or marketing department for all of the market data; you need some unbiased sources as well. As in journalism, you need some corroboration before you accept the data.
3. Include qualitative as well as quantitative information.
4. Collect the data using members of the strategy team. If they collect it, they will believe it. If a third party collects all of the data, the team will waste time picking it apart rather than using it.
5. Conduct some initial analysis on the data. The person or people who collect the data need to do this initial synthesis of it, i.e., "I saw this and I think we should consider doing that about it." Some new questions will arise that suggest the need for additional data. It is like being an investigative reporter; you follow the data trail until you come to a new place. Data collection draws the participant down the path of discovery. I call this phenomenon wallowing in the data until something new pops out.
6. Use the data for discussion. The initial analysis or recommendation is not the final strategy but the opening gambit for effective discussion. It gets the ball rolling for some exciting discussion.
7. Involve others. Data collection is not just limited to members of the strategy team. Though a team member is responsible for getting it done, he or she can and should involve others in the process. Involving others provides richer and more divergent data and energizes others in the organization about the potential for a new future.

The data-collection process provides facts to balance feelings, aids in developing consensus, and builds commitment to the final strategies. I have found that if people look at the same data, they will arrive at similar recommendations that aid in ensuring commitment and execution. To skip this step or blow through it quickly is like trying to build a skyscraper on a very shaky foundation. However, do not get caught in the trap of trying to obtain perfect data. It is not possible, and the attempt to do so could paralyze your efforts. Remember, 80 percent is close enough for horseshoes, hand grenades, and strategy development.

Discussion

Old style planning sessions often appear to be more a battle of positions than a true discussion where a constructive dialogue occurs about potential strategies. This battlefield approach is due in part to a lack of meaningful data as mentioned earlier. It is also because we have never been well educated in conducting meetings that allow for creativity and innovation. Most meetings are problem-solving meetings, there is an issue that needs fixing and the emphasis is on finding an acceptable solution as quickly as possible. Business education is chock full of ways and techniques to evaluate different alternatives. We are often too quick to use the tools once a couple of ideas have been thrown on the table. This rapid evaluation of a possibility is the fastest way to strangle the life out of any incipient idea before it has time to form, grow, and develop into something truly innovative and meaningful. A quick kill of an idea ensures that the issuer offers no more concepts, and the entire group will limit its discussion to those possibilities that can meet the initial scrutiny. This limits ideas to those that have worked in the past or are not too far away from what the company is doing now.

Strategies need to have some life breathed into them, be looked at from several perspectives, and opened up to additions and embellishments. In this way, the initial idea transforms into a new one, picking up support from the team as it goes. The final strategy may end up being quite different from the one that started the process. One way to resist the temptation to evaluate an idea too quickly is to have the team spend time articulating why an idea will work and the tangible benefits derived from it . . . the team just may surprise itself! Try this method with all ideas and more ideas are sure to jump out. Spend the majority of time expanding upon the list of ideas. You want to build as large a menu of potential strategies at this stage as possible. This discussion step sets up the third D.

Decide

Finally, we have come to the point where you can use all of those nifty techniques such as return on investment or economic value added. These analysis methods help you select and prioritize the alternatives. You may want to hold some strategies in reserve for a later time or as a back up if some strategies do not work out as planned. This is the time when consensus needs to be hashed out. The first two D's help build consensus along the way but now is where the rubber meets the road.

At this stage, you will not likely reach unanimity, so do not bother. Decision-making is not a democracy either. After all, though we may start meetings by saying that titles are left at the door, we all know that they are picked up again on the way out and some votes mean more than others. Full participation in the process is different from a majority vote. It is common and useful for the top manager to wait until he or she sees where the group's decision is going before making their own wishes known so as not to lead the witness as it were. Often, the chief executive will defer to the group rather than push his own view too hard. A good decision that the group endorses will be implemented far more effectively with better results than a better one that is driven by the executive only.

The top manager or chief executive enjoys and relishes giving the group its chance to lead rather than having to direct it. It is a wonderful opportunity to observe who can think out of the box and who looks strategically at the enterprise as a whole. It is an opportunity to be surprised by who does not rise to the challenge and by who blossoms and does rise to the challenge.

If you have difficulty reaching consensus, try the following definition of consensus. Consensus is where the majority understands, *agrees*, supports and implements the strategy. The minority understands, *accepts*, supports, and implements. The only difference between the two is accepting rather than agreeing. This need for understanding and acceptance is why the first two D's are so crucial to the process.

Now that consensus has been reached on the new innovative strategies you can proceed to the critical fourth D.

Definition of Consensus

Majority	Minority
Understands	Understands
Agrees	Accepts
Supports	Supports
Implements	Implements

Do

Now comes the hard part . . . the doing! The plan must be implemented and driven throughout the organization. The strategies must be assigned to a champion who will lead the charge and carry them out. It is critical that the champion is a member of the team that developed the plan. They understand it intimately, they committed to it and they are responsible for its implementation. The champion can get others involved and delegate parts of it, but somebody has to make sure it happens. The champion figures out the tactics, time frames, and resources needed to carry out the strategy. Though a lot of tactics may bubble out of the first two D's and should be noted, you do not want the entire team trying to micro-manage the details of a strategy.

Some strategies may naturally fall into a functional area, but most will involve other departments if the strategies are truly innovative and for the benefit of the entire organization. It is more important to select a champion who has the passion for the strategy than what functional area it falls into. Oftentimes the best champion will volunteer for the responsibility. They may need to be encouraged but should not be drafted into the effort or the strategy will find its way to the back burner on the to-do list.

Now its time for the fifth D. Yes, I misled you. There are really five. The four basic D's get you the plan, but a good plan is not static but dynamic. It can and should change if there are significant changes in the environment.

Deviate

The plan, when finished and documented, starts to become obsolete immediately. Some of the tactics for a strategy may not be effective and will change, which may cause a change in the timetable or the resources. People may leave the organization forcing a slowing of implementation until their replacements get up to speed. Some strategies may zoom ahead of plan. Current results may limit resources and slow the plan down. Though rare, a strategy may have to be abandoned or a new one added before the annual update of the strategy plan. The plan is a guide, directional in nature, to get substantive change initiated. It is not inflexible, written in stone, and blindly followed no matter what the consequences. It should not become a straightjacket but a way to measure and ensure progress on a new path.

The five D's are the basic components of a process for strategy development, a framework. All good planning processes incorporate the elements of the five D's.

Chapter 7

It Ain't Quite That Easy

D ue to the importance of the first D, data, this area deserves some additional exploration and discussion.

The Strategy Development Team

All of the five D's involve the members of the strategy development team. The team does the data collection. However, just who should be on this team? Normally the team consists of the head of the organization, the CEO, the president or general manager, all of his or her direct reports including head of sales, manufacturing, finance/accounting, human resources, information technology, research and development, quality, etc.

Ideally, the team should number eight to twelve people. If the team gets much larger, discussion time will increase geometrically and building consensus will take longer. On the flip side, you do not want the team to be too small which will limit the range of perspectives and opportunities. Too limited participation may result in low commitment to the final strategy plan, thus poor implementation. If you have to bend the rules on this, I would err on being more inclusive.

When selecting the team, include at least one voice of constructive discontent. You need to have one or two "Mikeys" on the team. Like the Mikey in the TV commercial for a cereal whose brothers say "Let Mikey try it. He never likes anything." Every organization has some Mikeys. Including one or more on the team increases the credibility of the final strategies with the rest of the organization and ensures that you will consider widely differing views. It also keeps you mindful that not everyone in the organization will automatically embrace the outcomes.

Be wary of loading the team with too many people from any one area. Often times a sales-oriented company will stack the team with people from that area. This stacking reduces the credibility that the plan is for the entire organization. It limits a balanced, cross-functional view of looking at the business as an entire system of interconnected and interrelated processes and people. This stacking can occur in any dominant area, not just sales.

The Internal Survey

A sample of the survey results is located at the back of the book in *Exhibit A*. Please take a few moments to re-view it now.

To collect a snapshot of the business today, we use an internal questionnaire called the Business Situation Analysis. This survey is completed by the strategy development team members. This particular version is set up for a manufacturer, but with some simple changes, it works quite well with any type of organization.

The survey is completely confidential and the information only used in aggregate form. We do request the individual's name but only to ensure that all surveys are completed and received. The surveys need to be sent to an independent entity for confidential compilation. Do not have anyone from the team or organization collect the surveys as this may be seen as opportunity to break the confidentiality of the individual responses. Give each respondent an addressed and postmarked envelope to send the survey in himself. I stress confidentiality with the surveys. If the survey is seen as truly confidential, the respondent will give very candid and honest answers. If it is not seen as confidential, then you will get carefully screened responses that are politically correct but may prove rather useless.

Exhibit A features not only some of the specific statements that the respondent rates from 1 to 10 in importance but also shows the format used to communicate the data back to the team. The exhibit shows an example of the subjects plus a few statements for each. Start with very general cross-organizational subjects and then work down to very specific areas and functions.

To the right of the statements, you will see a row of letters, each letter represents a respondent and the column underneath shows his/her responses. Further to the right, you will see the average score for that response. Next is a priority column with an A representing a big barnburner issue, a B representing a significant issue, and a C representing an issue that at least broke the barrier to be considered by the team. Last is the response percentage. This is important because a "0" response is not included in the calculation of the average since a "0" means no response or did not know.

By using the priority system, the team can quickly look for clusters of priorities in different areas and see where it needs to focus its attention. The results show the individual scores so members can see the strength of the responses. It is often worthwhile to delve further into those areas that may not have a high average but do have a bimodal distribution with a marked split between high and low numbers.

You may have noticed that all of the statements are said in a negative way. These statements are written intentionally this way for two reasons. First, we want to avoid what is called "Minnesota Nice," meaning if you cannot say something nice about somebody then do not say anything at all. Sorry, *strategy development is a contact sport* and it requires that everybody get the issues out on the table.

Secondly, it is a very efficient way to quickly see where the problems and opportunities lie. It is like a healthcare diagnostic tool. When you see the doctor, he does not ask you about all the areas where you feel fine but zeroes in on where you hurt, which is what this survey does. It does not matter what the organization's weaknesses are, every organization has them; just address them. They are a starting point to get you rolling.

Finally, we reach the fill in the blank questions. We use 217 numeric rating statements to help prepare the respondent to do a thorough job in filling out the write-in portions. If you simply ask people to write down their thoughts to open-ended questions without any prior stimulation, their answers will often be very brief and general in nature. It is unusual to rate an area as a high concern without having the other shoe drop, i.e., what they think should be done about it, which shows up in the written responses. A lot of very direct and exciting potential strategies start to bubble up in the written responses. It also gives people the opportunity to bring up subjects that are not covered in the numeric portion of the survey. Pet projects that no longer work, nepotism, and a variety of organizational conflicts often will surface in these written responses. These subjects are often the very obstacles and taboo issues that must be addressed in strategy development.

It is essential that all written statements, no matter how redundant, show up in the compilation. This shows the breadth and depth of the importance of the subject from the team's perspective. Naturally, some of the responses may need to be "sanitized" a bit, so that it is not apparent who made the statement or if it is offensive. For example, if the response is that the president is a tyrant and a dictator who never listens to anyone, it may show up as the president needs to work on his participative management and listening skills. Finally, never group the statements from one individual together. Mix them up a bit for confidentiality.

One last confidentiality tip—the row at the top of the format shows the respondents as individual letters. Individuals may spend a significant amount of time trying to figure out who is what respondent. Scramble the responses on the statements so there is no longer one column that represents the responses from one person. All the numbers are correct but the sequence is changed to protect the innocent. Spend the effort on anonymity to ensure that the team **focuses on the issue, not the issuer.**

Finally, this type of survey can be used with other groups within the organization beyond the strategy development team. You may survey the next level or two down in the organization or by functional department. It is useful to analyze different groups separately and compare the aggregate responses to see if they match up or vary to some degree. When there is a great deal of difference between groups, it may indicate poor communication between them or truly different perspectives. In either case, they need to be addressed in the strategy development process.

The SWOT Analysis

Many organizations seem to fall in love with a SWOT Analysis (identifies strengths, weaknesses, opportunities, and threats); yet, they do not get the true value from the exercise. It is usually done by the strategy development team members and it fills a lot of flip-chart sheets. There are lots of strengths and some weaknesses. The opportunities are seen as fixes for the weaknesses and the threats are that the company will not address the weaknesses! Unfortunately, the statement is not as fictitious as it sounds. Something close to this happens all the time.

Let us deal with strengths first. You can cut the list of strengths down by only including those that have direct value to your customers, meaning something they are willing to pay you for. Excellent products, quick delivery, great employees . . . these are tablestakes to be in the business. If you don't have them, you are out of the running! Pare the list down to the capabilities at which you truly excel. Then you will have identified your core competencies.

Correspondingly, not all weaknesses are truly weaknesses. They are not a weakness if the customer doesn't really care about them. All organizations have and will continue to have weaknesses; it is a waste of resources to fix those that do not matter to the customer. Why not spend the effort to ramp up valued strengths even further, making them insurmountable for the competition?

Opportunities are usually external to the company and are offered by the marketplace. Threats are always external to the company and should be dealt with only if they are both likely to occur and will have a significant impact on the success of the organization.

It is very easy to treat ourselves gently in a SWOT analysis. Companies have self-images just like people do. And just like people, they tend to be positive overall with a good dose of rationalization. Take me for example; I am not too heavy . . . I am just too short! I am the proper weight for a 7'1" basketball player. Look at the picture on your driver's license. Do you like it? That is the way you really looked to the camera that day. A good SWOT analysis is like the picture—it should reflect reality.

Let the external world be your lens for a compelling SWOT analysis. Utilize current customers, lost customers and potential customers to provide an accurate picture. Vendors and suppliers should also have input. These sources will add a dose of reality to your own perceptions. I am not saying a SWOT analysis is not useful. It just needs to be done as objectively as possible to get the best strategy development use out of it.

The Interviews

Another data-collection approach is to have the leader of the strategy development process or the facilitator conduct individual face-to-face visits with each member of the strategy development team. Some people feel more comfortable talking about issues and opportunities one on one than in a group setting. Some very sensitive issues or complex issues will surface that do not lend themselves to the write-in portion of the survey. It is also a time when the interviewee can think aloud about potential strategies.

I typically use the aggregate information from the survey as a guide for some initial questions to get the dialogue going in the interviews. I will ask, "What do you think of the groups' high response to this question?" Once you get rolling, the visit could easily last an hour or more. It is essential to listen closely, record all relevant points, and then elaborate on these points. This data, when used in aggregate, can add new issues and potential strategies to those from the survey. It also helps the interviewee start the journey in his thinking from the present to the future.

Again as with the surveys, you can solicit input from others in the organization beyond the strategy team. It may yield some new insights. Rather than one-on-one meetings, you may want to conduct the interviews in some small groups similar to a focus research group.

The Research Assignments

Success in creating new strategy is directly related to how well the organization is prepared for the strategy development sessions. In addition to surveys and interviews, a lot more data needs to be collected and analyzed. This step involves multiple data-collection assignments, analyzing both internal and external data. It is so critical that it deserves its own chapter.

Chapter 8

Learning from Your Own Successes and Failures and Those of Others!

Any time you begin a new journey, it is important to start at the beginning. It seems so self-evident it should go without saying. However, many organizations do not have an accurate picture of where their organization is now. Do we really know who our best, most profitable customers are? Are we all in agreement on them? Do we have the facts to back up our perceptions? We are so caught up in running the business that we fail to see how it has been changing ever so gradually and subtly over time. As pointed out so well in the book *Value Migration* by Slowotsky, customers' needs continually change. If you do not address these changes, customers will migrate to organizations that do. This migration phenomenon is especially true for businesses with reputations as leaders in their industries. They unintentionally end up being a legend in their own mind but less so in the eyes of their customers. Getting to the top is easy but staying there is difficult since everybody else is trying to beat you. Successful companies can become complacent and then they become less successful. Taking a hard look at the current state of affairs helps offset complacency and reveals new opportunities.

Below is a list of the type of exercises or research assignments that I use. They are generic enough to fit any organization with minimal adjustment and yet tailor themselves to your own organization. I will give some more thorough discussions to some of the key ones. We use all of them with clients since we want to

look in every nook and cranny for potential strategies and do it
from many different angles. We are continually surprised at the
areas from which a significant strategy pops out. Our list of
assignments is not the Holy Grail or the only way to do it.
However, the list does suggest fruitful areas for investigation. We
borrow from many different tools, authors and perspectives. You
should use whatever tools and approaches fit your own
organization. These examples may help you get started on
constructing your own process.

EXTERNAL ENVIRONMENT		
Research Assignment	*What it does*	*How the information is used*
Present and Potential Markets and Market Segments	Defines the customer types and basic characteristics of the customer types in each market segment identified. Characteristics include size, percent of business, growth potential, needs and expectations and threats.	Identifies potential segments for growth, key strategies for selling to segments, significant opportunities for new products and services to segments, and segments that should not be pursued and why.
Needs of Present and Potential Customers	Defines major customer groups, the products and services provided and indicates the quality, quantity and how vulnerable the product/service is to competition.	Also defines the products/services not provided, whether competitors offer the services and whether competitors are vulnerable. Identifies customer needs, how well the company and competitors are servicing those needs and what other needs could be served.
Competition Analysis	Defines major competitors and analyzes them based on market position and trend in market position, profitability, financial strength, product mix, technological capability, cost outlook, quality and product development. Identifies strengths and weaknesses in competitors.	This information is used to develop strategies that will capitalize on opportunities and reduce the impact of competitor threats.
Critical Industry/Company Issues	Defines issues critical to the industry and to the company's success.	Identifies strategies to resolve, minimize or capitalize on industry and company issues.
Key Industry Success Factors	Defines characteristics of strong industry or industry related players.	Identifies common characteristics for success in the industry to incorporate into strategies.

INTERNAL ENVIRONMENT		
Research Assignment	*What it does*	*How the information is used*
History Analysis—Review of Significant Events	Defines and analyzes the significant events that have taken place in the Company or affected the Company during the entire time it has been in business. Determine if these events had a positive or negative effect.	Identifies what type of past events have been successful or unsuccessful and why—so these can be carefully considered in planning for the future. In addition, it provides some insight into the driving force and values and philosophies of the Company.
Company Life Cycle Position	Defines the position the Company is at in its life cycle.	Identifies the type and extent of changes and emphasis that are needed to move toward a more desirable life cycle position (or maintain the present desirable one).
Organization Structure Evaluation	Defines the major organization structure weaknesses, gaps and problems that exist and may hinder the Company from implementing key strategies. Recognizes areas of strengths or areas the Company has not fully taken advantage of.	Identifies if the structure is in sync with the goals and strategies of the organization and the changes necessary to help the Company achieve them.
Financial History, Ratios and Trends	Develops comparative information for the Company for the past four years. Includes such items as number of employees, dollars invested in equipment, balance sheet and income statement items, and sales by product line. Compares these items to industry	Identifies major trends, shifts, changes and variances that may not be obvious based on a periodic review of the Company financial information. Corrective measures, improvement goals and other goals should be apparent when looking at this information.
Products and Services Analysis	Evaluates current products and services analyzing data on: sales and profits by product/service; present life cycle position; and potential threats or opportunities.	Helps to understand which products/services have contributed to the Company's growth in sales and profits. Determines how to handle products for future sales emphasis and capital investment.
Customer Profile Analysis	Defines major customers. Ranks them in descending order based on volume, gross profit dollars and gross margin percent. Indicates why the customer buys from the Company and the strength of the relationship.	Identifies which customers and customer types are opportunities for growth. Conversely, the analysis identifies which customer and customer types are weaknesses and may be costing the Company money.
Company Policies	Collects all major written and unwritten policies. Evaluates whether the policies will help or hinder the achievement of the Company's mission and strategies.	Identifies areas for policy clarification, additions or deletions.

Driving Force Analysis	Defines the Company's driving force using one of nine categories. A Company may have a primary and a secondary driving force. Examples of driving forces include products or services offered, market needs, technology, production capability, method of sal	Identifies the current driving force and analyze whether it needs to change or be enhanced by a secondary driving force.
Culture/Values Analysis	Defines the real values, philosophies and norms of the Company and determine if they are a strength or weakness.	Identifies cultural issues that may hinder or help in implementing the strategy plan. Also, recognizes values or philosophies that may have a major bearing on the Company's ability to change and achieve the plan.
Marketing Programs	Analyzes the strengths and weaknesses of the Company's current and past marketing programs. Focuses on market planning, product planning, advertising and promotional programs, and marketing information.	Identifies opportunities and threats related to this area.
Business Systems and Management Information Systems	Reviews and evaluates each of the Company's business systems and lists bottlenecks, problems and areas of concern. Defines the reporting process and determines if and how data is utilized.	Identifies any business system and management information problems that may be impediments and should be addressed in the planning process.

Question: After reviewing the list of internal and external research assignments, which areas do you need to collect more data from before beginning a strategy session?

Notes:

Chapter 9

Culture and Values Really Do Matter

When clients review our list of research assignments, they often feel that the culture and values assignment is soft or too "touchy feely" to really have an impact on their creation of strategy. They could not be further from the truth. An organization's culture and values have an extraordinary impact upon which strategies it will create and implement.

The values of an organization have a powerful effect, either positive or negative, on its current and future behavior. It is very subtle but strong. How often have you read reports about a new CEO that is appointed from outside the company only to read a year later that he has resigned due to a lack of chemistry with the company? This is culture and values at work . . . they can even take out a CEO!

Take the time to search out the values of your organization. If there is no explicit value statement, you can discern the true values by observing the behavior of the organization. Who does the organization promote and why? Who gets the perks and the rewards? What areas get the resources? What is frowned upon? Actions speak louder than words. The effort will uncover the true values operating in an organization irrespective of what may be printed.

The tricky thing about culture is that it is often articulated poorly internally and to the outside world. Many organizations such as GE, Target, Medtronic, and others have done an excellent job of communicating their values. They call these values guiding principles or beliefs. They may build them into their mission or vision statements. The key point is that the values are stressed and followed. More importantly, these companies strive to hire people who share the same value systems. Jack Welsh of GE fame has stated that if you hire the right people with the right values, you can teach them what they need to be successful on the job. On the other hand, someone with all the right experiences and talent that does not share your values will not be a success and is likely to leave the organization or be pushed out.

Problems can arise when a company is not aware of the values operating in the business and the values are contrary to what management wants or needs for future success. A company that is risk averse and rewards conformity isn't likely to develop significant new strategies. A company that is extremely optimistic and opportunistic, such as a high tech company, may chase so many opportunities that it is successful at none of them. Rather than sitting on its hands like the conservative company, it resembles the flight pattern of a butterfly!

Another hot spot can occur when a company's stated values are different from its actual day-to-day actions, which leads to frustration and discontent on the part of its employees. It's a case of management not walking the talk. This scenario can have more negative effects than not having any published values. Employees are quick to watch what behaviors are rewarded to discern the true values in operation. The company may say it values risk taking but penalizes those who fail. It may stress the importance of family but demands excessive work hours and looks down at absences due to family requirements.

Extol and reward values that are positive and useful and set in motion actions that will limit those that are not. And be patient; culture and value-system changes take time. It is a fast evolution, not a slow revolution. Do not make the mistake of trying to force it by hiring some new folks with radically new values just to shake the place up. Unless you protect these new folks or you hire a lot of them, they will either leave the organization due to the differences in values or they will slowly be converted to the existing ones. You are, in essence, trying to turn an ocean tanker that has a lot of momentum. It takes some time but it is very worth the effort.

It can get real scary when the organization is so new or has grown so rapidly in the number of employees that there is no value system or sense of culture in place at all. Each individual will work according to his values, which may be to the detriment of other employees and the company at large. The strength of value systems can keep companies out of trouble. A lot of corporate scandals can be laid at the doorstep of poor or no values systems. A company can gradually but quickly slide into trouble, something I call "Getting There in Grays."

Chapter 10

Getting There in Grays

Most folks are appalled with the recent and seemingly endless revelations of corporate misconduct and criminal behavior at some of the largest and previously respected business organizations. Directors, top management and bankers, lawyers, brokers, and accounting firms are under investigation or have been indicted for everything from SEC violations, criminal fraud and theft, to obstruction of justice.

We shake our heads and ask, "How could they do this?" "Can anyone be this stupid or incompetent?" "Are there no longer any bounds to greed, ego and arrogance?" What we safely can assume is that these individuals didn't wake up one morning, look in the mirror and consciously decide to become criminals. They got to this lowest level of corporate behavior in a long series of small, downhill steps into the black abyss. They got there in grays.

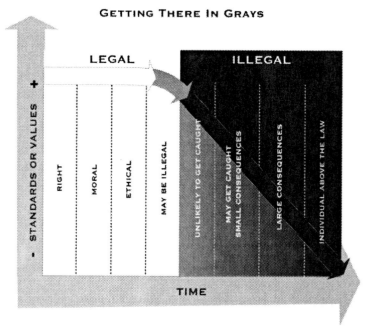

GETTING THERE IN GRAYS

At the reputable end of the scale of values and standards chart are many organizations and people who do the right thing just because it is the right thing to do. Many of these organizations and people are right in your own backyard. They might be highly involved in their community or contribute to charities. They far exceed society's expectations.

Next are those who have a strong moral compass that keeps them within society's norms, followed closely by those with impeccable ethical standards that are both written and followed. All of these organizations operate in what's known as the "White Zone."

Nearby, however, lurks a large "Gray Zone," its area of which "May Be Illegal." The Gray Zone is based on the "interpretation" of laws and regulations. It is the firmament of a countless army of advisors such as law and accounting firms, consulting organizations, banks and brokerage houses.

These so-called outside advisors are paid handsomely to pack as much questionable business activity as possible into this area, all the while insulating the culprits from scrutiny from within or without. Phrases like "At least we have something to hang our hat on" or "It hasn't been proven to be illegal" are bandied about as if they are gospel. In reality, this is the beginning of the slippery slope down into the "Black Illegal" zone.

Unfortunately, even this illegal zone is sliced and diced into small pieces to make the journey more palatable. The first step down is the "Unlikely to Get Caught" area. Due to limited visibility or scarce enforcement resources, the risk of getting caught is low.

The next step down is "May Get Caught" but the consequences are small. It may mean a cease and desist ruling or a small fine or regulatory slap on the wrist. It is quite easy to move into the next level, "May Get Caught," and the consequences here are considerably larger, such as a seven-figure fine. Many believe, however, that the financial gains far outweigh the costs. For example, a $2-million fine for polluting may be seen as a cost of doing business when compared to tens of millions of dollars in profits.

Finally, one hits the bottom of the black pit; the "no matter how bad the consequences are for the business, I will not be held personally responsible." This is where one considers themselves above the law. One may feel they will never be charged or at least not convicted. The blame can be passed on to outside advisors or other managers. One will often plead ignorance or in this last stage, the Fifth Amendment.

As an individual or organization takes each step down, pauses, and then nothing bad happens, this lower level becomes the norm from which one can proceed further down the slope. The distance from one step down to the next is hardly noticed, except for the increased money or false profits.

But over time, enough small steps will eventually and inevitably lead to the final reckoning. It's only a matter of time. Once the habit of getting away with it starts, the behavior becomes addictive and is difficult to reverse. Momentum builds as the slope increases and the gravity of the action grabs hold until the bottom looms, too late to reverse course.

The concept of "Getting There in Grays" applies far beyond business settings. How many of us get increasingly aggressive on our tax returns each year? How many of us believe that a 65 mph speed limit means we can pass the police at 72 mph with impunity or simply get a warning at 75 mph? How many people drink modestly, drive home and arrive safely, and then decide to drink a little more the next time?

We need to continuously pause to re-evaluate our standards and values to avoid slow, subtle and incremental deterioration. We never want to reach the stage where we look back and ask, "How did I ever get to this sorry state?" It is far too easy to get there in grays.

Chapter 11

Managing Your Human Capital and the 20-60-20 Rule

The number of strategy plans I see that encompass very new and innovative strategies but do not take into consideration the change in human resources that will be required to carry out the strategies is amazing to me. Training and education may need to occur as well as the securing of some new and different talents.

Update Training and Talents

An example of this concept is the strategic shift large traditional retail stock brokerage companies went through when online trading became widespread and inexpensive. The large firms resisted this change for years until a new entrant to the industry, Charles Schwab, changed the rules and achieved great success.

The large brokerage companies realized that the practice of charging 7 percent commission on trades was no longer a viable business model and moved to charging a much smaller percentage to manage an individual's portfolio, thus aligning their revenue stream with the success of the client's investment success.

The challenge for the brokerage houses was that their brokers' high incomes were based upon the high commissions on transactions. As a result, their brokers were very good at generating a lot of transactions. Unfortunately, this practice sometimes encouraged the promotion of excessive trading. The new strategy came as quite a shock to the brokers, requiring them to focus now on the long-term success of their clients' investments and required a more customer-focused adviser approach. The companies undertook extensive comprehensive training to reorient their brokers to the new business model. After significant time and effort, they were able to make the conversion. However, they lost a significant number of their very seasoned, high-income senior brokers who just could not make the shift . . . they were traders at heart.

It is interesting to observe the circle of change continuing. As online trading fell off dramatically with the bear stock market of three-plus years, online discount brokerages have started to provide advisory services to their clientele.

You do not have to wait until you develop significant new strategies to evaluate your human resource capital. Many companies find that not all of their employees are able to execute the current business plan effectively, which brings me to the concept of the 20-60-20 rule of human resources.

20/60/20 Rule

Most managers are familiar with the 80-20 rule where 80 percent of the volume comes from 20 percent of your customers. A variation of that rule is the 20-60-20 rule in the productivity and effectiveness of all of your employees in every area, including management.

Up to 20 percent of your people are top performers, often in spite of your efforts. For example, your list of top 20 percent in sales performers probably does not change much from year to year. Excellence is part of their normal way of life . . . they strive to find new ways to grow in their careers. They often perform so well, so consistently and quietly that they are taken for granted.

Correspondingly, the bottom 20 percent will be poor performers no matter how much time and effort you spend on them. It doesn't mean they are not nice people; it is just that they do not have the ability or desire to excel in their current positions. Unfortunately, management often spends too much time on these folks. Yet, the acceptance of their substandard performance sends a bad signal to the remaining 80 percent that poor performance is tolerated or accepted. They pull everyone else's motivation, especially the middle 60 percent, down. They also irritate the top 20 percent who feel they must carry this baggage along.

The middle 60 percent are good, solid performers day in and day out. They are the backbone of any good organization. Not everyone can be a top performer nor does a company need that as long as it treats each category of the 20-60-20 appropriately.

The Top 20 Percent

The first category to address is the top performers. These are the very people that your competitors and other companies would love to get their hands on. Unfortunately, not only is this group not given the amount of attention they deserve, they are often undercompensated relative to the value they provide to the business. Besides rewarding them appropriately, why don't we model after them?

Many people scoff at the concept of using top performers as models for the organization because they may be seen as prima donnas that don't follow the rules. This is probably true since top performers will not waste their time on low impact items or inefficient processes and paper work. They intuitively search out better ways of doing their business. Let's put our emotional investment in the current practices aside and look at what they are doing and accomplishing, change our practices accordingly and teach them to the rest of the organization!

Other people say we cannot model after Wally or Wanda because that is just the way they are. They have the right attitudes, aptitudes and motivation to be top performers no matter what the circumstances. I agree that they have "the right stuff," but can't we change our hiring practices and profiles to attract more of these people? It is worth the effort to try because the payoff can be so big.

Make the most of your top performers. Compensate them to ensure you keep them. Model your processes after theirs and hire more like them.

The Bottom 20 Percent

Now, on to the second group to address—the poor performers. These are the people that management usually spends about 80 percent of their interpersonal time on. A nasty perversion of the 80-20 rule! No matter how much time you spend with them, they just do not seem to get it! They have, in effect, slowly and gradually, and almost imperceptibly, lowered the bar of performance over the years.

You must develop a plan of corrective action for these employees and managers. First, set the expectations for minimum standards of performance. It may surprise some people to find out they are on the bottom of the performance scale. Sure they may have been coasting for a couple of years but they never got fired or reprimanded for it. They received decent reviews and pay raises, so everything must have been all right. They may have even changed departments since a common response to this deterioration of performance is to "put lipstick on a pig" where one manager falsely sings their praises and passes them on to some other unsuspecting manager!

The first step in dealing with poor performers is to ensure that the person is truly a poor performer and the label is not based on attitudes and perceptions that have subjectively built up over the years. Once a person has been labeled as a poor performer, it is a view that is tough to overcome even if the person has since improved gradually over time. It is essential that you verify and substantiate the poor performance. You may not like these people, but if they perform and meet the standards, that is all you can ask. Remember these standards will be used to track progress, and, if necessary, used as a basis for termination later on, so the assessment of performance needs to be correct for the employee's sake, and so the company does not expose itself to potential litigation if there is a termination. The minimum standards must be objective and apply to the entire group the employee is in. Include quantitative as well as quantitative standards.

This is the time when "evaluation inflation" rears its ugly head. It is a natural human emotion to avoid conflict and hurting a person's feelings. When you review their personnel file, you may be surprised to find that you and previous managers have been giving them acceptable performance evaluations and salary increases. This trend has to be stopped and reversed immediately.

The next step is to develop their improvement goals, setting a specific timetable for reaching them with benchmarks along the way. A thirty-sixty-ninety-day timetable should be enough time to reach the minimum standard. A plan of supporting actions by the manager and the organization must be developed to help the person meet the standards. Do they have the right training? Do they need new tools to work with to get the job done? Periodic coaching sessions to help them along are also required.

The rest is up to them. If they reach the standards expected, they are now a productive member of the team. If not, then they need to find a new home where they can be successful either inside the organization or outside of it!

Another point to keep in mind is that reformed poor performers are not allowed to drop back down below the standards once the pressure is off—that is grounds for release. Unfortunately, some poor performers have learned to improve performance while they are under scrutiny and fall back into their old ways once the heat is off. Another tactic reformed poor performers use is to hunker down until their manager moves on. A lot of inadequate performers have managed to outlive a lot of managers, especially in businesses that are growing and have a lot of internal promotions.

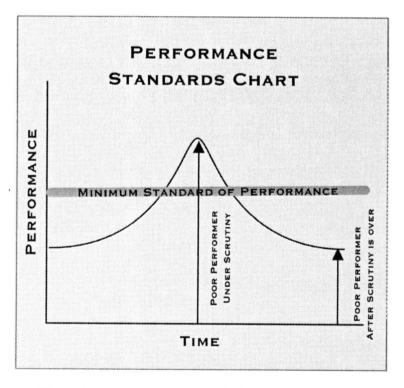

The main reason managers avoid addressing poor performers is that no one likes to terminate an employee. Robert Townsend, in his book *UP the Organization*, states that this is the single most avoided management responsibility. Yet, it is a crucial one. Employees need two things to be successful . . . the ability to do so and the desire to do so.

It is far easier to fire the person with the lack of desire or a poor attitude. It is far tougher to release the person that is well liked and tries hard. We all know who these people are in our organization. They are the ones who volunteer to arrange, run and clean up after the company picnic. They come to work early, work hard and leave late. They are good at everything but their job. The other tough fire is people who have been successful under the old strategies but cannot be effective with the new strategies. It is not kind to leave them in their current spot. You are letting their value and marketability deteriorate so that if the business slows and the day of reckoning occurs, they have a tough time showing potential employers what value they brought to your organization. It is far better to help move them along quickly to a different organization that has different requirements they can meet and be successful. I may be "pollyanna-ish" but I think every one can be successful somewhere. Help them get there!

Terminate the person with dignity and respect; for their benefit, the benefit of the department employees they are leaving, and your organization. These people will move on to other companies in the future and will share their experiences and perceptions with others. Terminate them the way you would want to be terminated. You likely will be terminated some day, too.

The Middle 60 Percent

Recognizing the top 20 percent and taking corrective action on the bottom 20 percent can truly re-energize the middle 60 percent. It is the middle 60 percent that have the greatest potential for increased productivity resulting in increased bottom-line profitability because there are so many of them. They realize that top performers are well rewarded and poor performance is no longer acceptable. The bar has been raised and they will move to meet or exceed it. Given the choice, the training and the tools, most people prefer to move towards the top.

Most of the clients I have worked with utilized this approach and achieved outstanding results. Roughly half of the bottom 20 percent (10 percent) of the population significantly improved their performance. Of the remaining 10 percent, half (5 percent) are replaced with new, better performers; hopefully folks that will make it into the top-performer category. The last 5 percent are found to have been so unproductive that they are not replaced at all! This saves 5 percent of the payroll to reallocate elsewhere, with some of it going to the top performers. Keeping the top 20 percent while improving the productivity of 75 percent (middle 60 percent + 10 percent that now meet the minimum standards + 5 percent new replacements), and saving 5 percent of the payroll is a winning combination!

Most managers on the strategy development team understand and support this approach once it is laid out and they know that everyone will follow the same path. What they may not realize is that this approach needs to be used at all levels in the organization, including their own. You cannot address just the middle and lower ranks of the organization. The most leverage is achieved when it is applied from the top to the bottom! The least acceptable area for poor performance is at the senior management level because it has such a tremendous impact on those employees that report to a poor manager.

So if you are part of a senior management team of five people and the other four look real effective . . . watch out! Look in the mirror and reassess your own performance!

Naturally, the percentages of top, middle and poor performers will vary by organization but the idea of utilizing a bell curve and addressing the grouping of employees on a periodic basis is a very effective one. Seriously consider a little MIT (Management Initiated Turnover) to jump-start your resources!

HUMAN CAPITAL — THE 20 - 60 - 20 RULE		
What We Actually Do		*What We Should Do*
• Underpay them • Take them for granted • Do not fully benefit from their skill and expertise	**TOP PERFORMERS** **20%**	• Reward and compensate for value provided • Model their behavior • Hire more to their profile • Give the recognition warranted
• De-motivate them with the toleration of the bottom 20% and the attention poor performers receive • Not enough focus on the solid performers	**SOLID PERFORMERS** **60%**	• Raise the performance standards • Address poor performers • Focus more time on developing potential • Show a performance culture
• Waste too much time on them • Overpay for their value • Not effectively addressed in the short or long term	**POOR PERFORMERS** **20%**	• Put in place objective minimum standards of performance • Put poor performers on improvement plan • Replace those that do not improve

A Bit of a Digression

There are many great programs and books available on effectively hiring and terminating employees that can provide the education and training in these processes that many managers lack. However, I want to share a philosophy I learned many years ago as a sales manager regarding hiring and firing.

Many managers practice a *quick hire/slow fire approach*. Because a job may have been open for a while and the work is backing up, managers speed up the hiring process and select only an acceptable candidate. They may not spend enough time training and coaching them, so when 12 months pass and the person is ineffective they feel a bit guilty and give them more time. Eventually, when they can take the poor results no longer (say 18 months) they finally let the person go and start all over. Just think, 18 months of frustration and ineffectiveness!

Reverse the practice! Use a *slow hire/quick fire* approach! Be patient, take the time to do it right. The gap in time may be painful but far less so than hiring a candidate that doesn't work out. Also, recognize that no matter how thoroughly you may test and interview and research a candidate, it still is a roll of the dice and you may only have a 50-50 chance of success on the first try. This is why it is so

---

Use a slow hire/quick fire approach for better hiring results

---

critical that you set up a probationary program of say 30-60-90 days with performance benchmarks. If the candidate is a poor match, you deal with it quickly for both his and your company's benefit.

This concept may seem harsh but is necessary to offset our natural distaste to fire anyone since it is painful and unpleasant. We often will hide the truth form ourselves. When working with a construction company on the 20-60-20 issue, the strategy development team agreed with the system. However, they tried to duck the issue by saying they had to wait on a new human resource performance tracking system to identify poor performers and it would not be up and running for about nine months. I asked each of the eight managers, each representing different functional areas, to write on a slip a paper the names of the top three and bottom three project managers out of a group of twelve. Each manager had identical listings! They knew all along the poor performers, they just needed to verify it objectively.

I use a simple system to determine when to start the process of improving or terminating a person that I learned from a friend of mine who owned some show horses. He asked his trainer and stable owner, "How do you know when it is time to geld a stallion so he will calm down and be manageable?" Gelding is a big step and irreversible, so it is not taken lightly and often avoided too long. The trainer replied, "When the thought first crosses your mind!" He knew that most owners do not want to admit that it needs to be done and try to rationalize away the inevitable. It is much the same way with a new hire or poor performer. When the thought first crosses your mind about releasing someone, start the process rolling.

By now you must be thinking, enough of this human capital stuff. My reason for hitting it so hard is simple. No matter how great your strategies may be, they will only get implemented through the combined efforts of all of your employees. Your employees are a crucial piece of the strategy game plan. I truly believe that your most effective advantage is your people. Any organization can acquire hard assets such as buildings and equipment; it is the quality, motivation and capabilities of your employees that determine how effectively you utilitize them!

Question: What steps can you take to align your human resources with your strategies?

Notes:

Chapter 12

Business Information Systems—
Lots of Data but
Little Management Information

Information reporting grows quicker than a bunch of rabbits in mating season. We are awash in a sea of green-and-white paper or disks that back up online data. It happens so easily. An ad hoc report all of a sudden becomes monthly and so as not to leave anyone out of the loop, more and more people are added to the distribution list. Then one recipient modifies it a little and on it goes . . . the information explosion taking on a life of its own, killing more trees as we go. It is not much different with everything online now; it just clutters our e-mail and electronic filing systems. A thorough review of your management information system will allow you to streamline it. Reduce the volume of data while improving accuracy and speed of delivery. What is needed is the right amount of accurate information at the right time.

The power of today's computers and their proliferation throughout organizations provides mountains of data at management's fingertips. We are spoiled by this ready access to the latest sales figures, shipment numbers and cost data and may spend too much time analyzing the past, rather than plotting out our course for the future.

Historical data is just that . . . its history. It tells you what has happened and where you have been. It is useful; it helps to point out past trends. However, we live in the present and try to influence our future. What can be done to reverse a negative trend or amplify a positive one? This is the true stuff of management creativity and leadership.

Overuse of historical data is like trying to drive a car by only looking at the view through your rearview mirror rather than looking ahead through the windshield. In planning the future, you want to not only look at the car ahead, but also the car several blocks ahead.

Hard numeric or statistical data analysis must be complemented with less precise information from the external world to guide you to the best possible future. What are the industry trends, new technologies, new competitors, and new product developments? How is the profitability of customers changing? These less quantifiable parameters will have far more impact on your business than last week's shipments. Information collection and analysis in these areas needs to be as thorough and timely as inside data.

Remember, if you spend all of your time looking inward at historical data, it means you have your posterior aimed at your customers and the external world.

But don't throw out those reams of green-and-white paper just yet or purge those data files. The information is valuable; it just needs to be managed in a timely and concise manner.

First, limit the information overload to those key indicators that tell you how well the organization is doing. You probably need less than a dozen or so. If an indicator looks bad, then you can dig in the area in more detail rather than wallowing in a mess of details trying to make sense of it all. These key indicators work like the instrument gauges on a plane, boat, or car. A quick glance lets you know all systems are running in the green.

Secondly, make sure the data is timely. Often, reports from accounting are reported too slowly or in large aggregate amounts. Typically, information is presented a week or two after the close of the month. That can be six weeks away from a significant shift in orders, shipments, or purchases. Set up flash reports that are weekly (or daily) that help you quickly determine the health of the business.

Thirdly, put the data in perspective—is it a blip or part of a trend? If you are not sure, dig deeper or monitor it more frequently. A bad week of order entry is a blip, especially if it is followed by strong ones. However, two poor weeks suggests you are in the yellow zone of this scanning instrument or gauge and three poor weeks means the needle is moving into red.

Finally, take decisive action when your gauges are running in the red. Small, timely corrections and adjustments help keep the machine running smoothly. And just like in a plane, the internal gauges are important, but it's more important to look out the windshield to ensure you are staying on course. In a car, even on a straight road, some minor corrections are needed to keep you out of the ditch. With the increasing velocity of business in today's marketplace, you need to quickly ascertain how the organization is doing (internal data) so you can spend the time guiding the organization in the external world. Otherwise, speed can truly kill.

Examples Of An Information Systems Review

To give you a feel for the types of benefits that you can realize from a thorough management information review I will give you two client examples.

The first company is a large franchisee for a fast food chain with several dozen restaurants. The management information assignment was completed by the CEO who had a strong information technology and financial background. He got carried away. He presented a fifty-two-page report to the strategy development team . . . talk about missing the point on streamlining! He was sent back to pare the report down to three pages that everyone could understand. When he did, he discovered that each restaurant

---

Management Data Requirements

Concise
Accurate
Timely

counted 115 items in inventory each week. It took three days to assemble and send the data in to headquarters and worse yet, it was rarely used because it was almost a week late.

They realized they only needed to count fifteen items for a flash report that could be available the next day and would indicate how each restaurant was doing. It was labor saving, more accurate, more timely and most importantly, it was used!

The second example is of a distribution company that sold to hundreds of convenience stores. It found that 25 percent of its invoices were at no charge! Marketing was using the invoice system to track promotional racks. Moreover, they were sending multiple invoices to the same store. They did this to track sales by department; originally, they only sold into one department or two versus seven at the time. Worst of all, they sent invoices to all individual stores even if they were part of chain, which forced the chain to aggregate them . . . not great customer service!

The situation appears to be somewhat unbelievable, but it is not really all that unusual. Information and system changes get layered on to the system gradually over time, like the layers of an onion. Each change made sense in and of itself but eventually grew into a monstrosity. By stopping using invoices to track racks, including all departments on one invoice and billing chains in aggregate, they reduced their processing costs by more than 35 percent and reduced the aging of their receivables significantly. They improved their bottom line by over half a million dollars the first year with just this one change!

A thorough management information system review can improve productivity and the bottom line while improving customer value and take a lot of stress out of the operation.

Question: What key data indicators do you need to tell you business is on track? Do you receive this information now in a timely, accurate, and easy-to-process manner?

Notes:

Chapter 13

Business Is Like a Bicycle

When working with clients on strategy development, I often draw a parallel between a business and a bicycle. The front wheel is the directional wheel made up of customers and markets the company serves and the products and services they offer. The back wheel is the mechanism that delivers the goods to the customer. This back wheel represents areas of operations, production and delivery. It is the force of power and movement forward. In business, nothing is concretely accomplished unless the product or service is provided and billed. The pedals, chains, sprockets and gears are the staff functions that are so important to link the front wheel and the back wheel into a coherent system. Lastly, the seat represents the important human resource that powers the entire system.

If the front wheel is not aimed in the right direction or turns left and right a lot, it's difficult to make good forward progress towards your goal. The wheel does need to be re-aimed periodically to avoid obstacles or a road that would run you in a circle. This task is the function of sales and marketing. The key point of this analogy is that if the wheel is too small or has a flat tire or is aimed in the wrong or no direction, it does not matter how hard you pedal; you will not make progress, and worse yet, could crash or fall over.

If you are not aimed at the right customers and markets, it does not matter how efficiently and effectively your operation runs. You are in deep weeds. This is why it is so important that you do a superb job in data collection on the front wheel subjects. Over 60 percent of your strategy development efforts should be spent on the areas of customer/markets and products/services. If these areas are aimed properly, then it is easier to focus the operational and support strategies that are needed to deliver the goods and services.

For this reason, I will give a glimpse of the research (data collection) assignments we use to help address these areas, and the types of issues and outcomes you can expect to encounter.

The Customer Profile

The first assignment we focus on is the customer profile. The assignment asks you to rank all of your customers using the following four variables:

- Annual sales volume in descending order for the past three years
- Annual gross margin dollars in descending order for the past three years
- Gross margin percentage in descending order for the past three years and
- The ease of doing business with them

For the first three steps, the outcomes are obvious. The ease of doing business or degree of difficulty in working with a customer drives at all of the costs of doing business with a customer. Such costs include excessive customer service, sales or design help, holding inventory for them, slow payment, excessive returns and so on. An activity based costing system (ABC) will give you most of the information.

These four categories will give you a good snapshot of the present state of affairs. It is essential that you have a good grasp of what is before you start brainstorming what can be.

If you have never done this before, you are likely to find some interesting surprises! A construction product supplier found that the top 350 customers out of 1,500 provided 120 percent of their gross profit dollars. That is right—120 percent. They could not believe it at first and rechecked the figures. They were accurate. On further investigation, they found that the remaining 1,150 customers were sucking up all of their customer service, and sales and design resources. This distribution of resources inflated these service costs which were being borne by their best customers!

The company was, in effect, overcharging their best customers relative to the services they used in order to cover the costs of the poor ones. This situation can be the kiss of death in a highly competitive market. Even worse, their smaller customers and orders were gumming up the factory causing long delivery cycles, more rejects and lower overall quality. Talk about the 80-20 rule coming home to roost!

Now the question is: What do you do with the unprofitable customers you discover? First, you may get them into the profitable zone by either cutting costs through reduced service levels or increasing profitability through price increases. Another approach is to streamline processes in dealing with these accounts. You will be stunned to see how often either or both of these strategies will work without losing the customer.

Let's look at another example. The travel business runs on razor-thin margins. One large travel company we worked with spent a lot of money providing detailed travel reports to its larger clients. Sales people were paid a commission on the gross sales so they ended up throwing in all of the company's services in order to secure the business, including these reports. When the sales peoples' compensation was better aligned with the company's objectives with commission based on a client's gross margin, they quickly discovered that the reports were not important to the big clients who utilized their own in-house reports. Dropping these expensive reports not only saved money but also streamlined operations.

Yes, some customers may leave you as a result of these changes in tactics but that will be good for them and for you. They will find a new supplier that better matches their requirements and you will have "fired" a customer that is not profitable. Remember you cannot be all things to all people no matter how hard you may try. We often mislead ourselves by the feeling that any increase in volume is good, especially if you have a lot of high fixed costs in plant and equipment. Remember, only profitable increases in volume are good increases!

The Product Profile

Our product profile asks the client to do essentially the same things as in the customer profile when they rank the products or services from top to bottom by:

- Sales volume
- Gross margin dollars
- Gross margin percentage
- Degree of difficulty in working with the product line.

It also asks that a product life cycle curve be completed on each major line or product. Again, the results can be rather startling.

You may find that some products have declined so much over time that they should be eliminated or rejuvenated if possible. You may also discover that you are not providing enough resources to emerging new products. With mature products, are you providing a level of resources that can keep the core of your product line strong? It is too easy to take the solid workhorses for granted and not reinvest enough in them.

Every company must face the issue of what to do with poor performing or unprofitable products. The tactics covered earlier in the customer profile apply. Yes, there is strong resistance to dropping a product or service with a plethora of excuses offered. The best one and the most fallacious is "it doesn't cost anything to keep it in the line" or "let's keep it in until we use up the inventory." It costs real money in inventory, counting inventory, catalog space and expense, literature, etc. to keep very slow movers.

And do not forget Mr. Murphy and his law! If you have twenty-five machines for sale in stock and it is a year or more supply, you may desire to keep it in the line. But as inventory dribbles down to four, you will suddenly get an order for six. You do not have enough parts inventory to make the remaining two, and the minimum order for the most expensive parts is fifty units. Now you are forced to disappoint a customer (Murphy will be sure to make sure it is a big volume one). Do not fall into this trap! If your analysis says drop it . . . drop it. Notify customers ahead of time of the remaining inventory. Sell it on a first-come, first-serve basis and the inventory will make its way out the door. If it is an industrial component, be sure to give customers time to find an alternate supplier.

Dropping product is difficult for companies to do. Due to the inherent predisposition of sales and marketing to add, not drop, products, this continual review to avoid product line proliferation should be assigned to operations. They are aware of which products and services are the most and least profitable. A helpful process point is to assume that after the analysis, all of the recommendations by operations to drop products are accepted. Leave it up to sales and marketing to argue them back into the lineup. Remember, it is OK to have a dog or two in the line. You just do not want to run a kennel!

One never knows what new strategies will pop out of an analysis like this one. One client discovered to their sorrow that over 80 percent of their new products were not truly new at all. The client was caught in a cycle of creating modified products that did not provide much in new sales or profits even though they had a staff of eighty-plus new product engineers. They put in processes to force a more thorough evaluation of the net new potential of product endeavors, which cut their list of projects by 65 percent. They also split apart their engineering department into three sections. The three sections represented product modifications, product customizations for specific customers and truly new products. They learned that the skills and aptitudes for each of these areas are quite different as well as the time frames and resources required.

The customer profile and products and services analyses help look at your front wheel today. Making sure you know where you are now will often lead you to where you want to be in the future.

Pulling It All Together

We often combine the data from the customer profile and product services profile in a graphic way using the Customer/Market-Product/Service grid shown below. Plotting products and services in this grid allows the strategy development team to visualize all of the organization's current efforts and suggest future strategies.

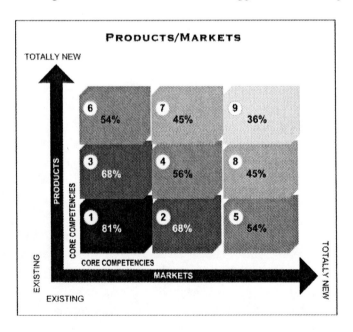

Box #1 represents the company's core competencies in the market place. Boxes #2 and #3 show the newer growth approaches, with the farther out boxes indicating effort farther out in the future or further away from the core competencies. The percentages of likely success in each box are only approximate, based upon various studies and articles, and may actually be somewhat optimistic. They are provided only for illustrative purposes to show that the further away an effort is from core competencies, the lower the odds for success.

Naturally, totally new customers or markets involving totally new products and services (represented by Box #9) requires a much larger and longer learning curve and investment for the company, thus lowering the odds for success. Box #9 represents a difficult undertaking unless these efforts are in the form of an acquisition of a company that has capabilities in these areas. Even then, such an acquisition has significant risks.

Boxes #2 and #3 are equally attractive efforts that leverage off of your strengths. What you want to avoid is playing the old game of twister where you have to put your hands and feet into various boxes based on a roll of the dice. This game extends you and puts you off balance until you fall. You do not want to spread your resources too thin at any given time. Your primary effort may be Box #2 with a secondary effort in Box #3. Just do not put equal effort into both. It is like a prizefighter in action; he leads with a jab and strikes with the hook, the big punch. You never see a fighter try to land a big punch with both hands at the same time. It is unbalanced and makes you very vulnerable!

This exercise will usually create a lot of good arguments about what products and services are in each of the boxes and where your true strengths lie. Some companies are surprised to find out just how many boxes they are dabbling in. This surprise is common to companies that are encountering financial difficulty. It also represents the typical turnaround strategy of getting out of the far-flung efforts that are sapping the organization of resources and taking away from the core business.

As you look to grow beyond Box #1, remember the next box you may be entering may be a core competency or a Box #1 for a competitor. They may not be happy to see you there! It is useful to place your competitor's customers/markets and products/services on another grid. This analysis may indicate where there are few or weak competitors which allows greater opportunities for success. It will also show areas where you cannot prevail because there is the proverbial 800-pound gorilla (competitor) you do not want to mess with! Keep competitors in mind as you look to grow.

Sometimes it is enticing to try something new, especially if Box #1, 2 or 3 are not high growth or "sexy." Unfortunately, the outlying boxes take the time of the best executives while leaving the core relatively unattended. If the "cash cow" of the core begins to deteriorate, then, "Katie, bar the door!" Things can unravel pretty quickly in today's fast-paced marketplace. It is a matter of managing the current business well while building for the future.

Even though I have focused on the front wheel in the products and markets examples, you should not ignore the rest of the departments and areas (the rest of the bicycle). Creative strategies should be developed for all areas of the organization. After all, if you only have a front wheel, you have got a unicycle . . . not a very efficient way to make progress.

Question: What customer needs are not being met now? How can you find out additional needs of customers?

Notes:

Chapter 14

Where Do I Start?

Once you have done all the initial data collection and are ready to start the strategy development sessions, it is essential that you start at the right place in your discussions. The best starting component of the typical strategy plan is not where folks traditionally start!

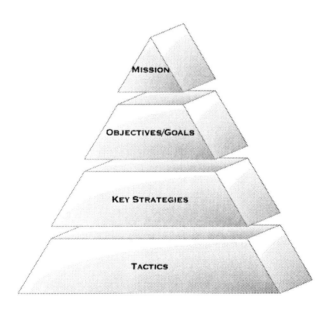

Most organizations have a tendency to start at the apex of the triangle—the mission statement. If one does not have a mission statement, you could spend four or more hours on it and end up with motherhood and apple pie, and a bunch of frustrated participants. This results from not having done the basic strategy work on who your best customers and products are, and who they should be, and how you will mesh them together . . . critical components of the mission statement. Conversely, if you have a reasonably good mission statement, it may artificially limit you from looking into other exciting opportunities. To avoid these two scenarios, do not start with the mission statement!

A second but misguided starting point is with the goals and objectives, which is to start with the end in mind. I call this approach backing into the numbers. Unfortunately, no one knows if they are the right numbers. Are they realistic? Do they have too much stretch in them? Are they too conservative? It is impossible to tell unless you know what strategies will be employed to reach them. Sessions often denigrate into heated debate about the validity of the numbers based on each individual's own perspective. Sales may be very conservative (I can say this from my own experience as a sales manager . . . I never set a goal or objective that I could not easily hit!) and accounting may be too aggressive trying to please the stakeholders. In both cases, they are most likely wrong.

If the numbers are decided upon first, then the rest of the sessions will be spent on how to back into the numbers. This usually entails just moving the numbers on a Projected Profit and Loss Statement, up and down a little bit here and there. But remember what I said earlier about projections . . . at their worst, they are a fiction, or at the most, a best guess! You will fall into the classic trap of doing last year harder. Most organizations and their people are already running flat out. A majority of managers are already working fifty to sixty hours a week and more. They cannot work harder . . . they must work smarter with new approaches and new strategies. One definition of insanity is to do the same exact thing but expect different results, so let us stop the corporate insanity of doing last year harder.

> **Strategy drives the numbers,**
> **not the reverse!**

A third approach is to have the strategy team tackle the tactics first. It usually starts with a memo from the president asking all department heads to come up with their plans for the next year and, by the way, to think strategically. So everyone forecasts conservatively on their results and asks for significant increases in resources . . . the classic budgeting game. In tallying these "plans" from the individual departments, no discernible significant strategies appear, yet the budget requests far outstrip the results offered. In frustration, the president passes it on to the controller to make sense of it all. The controller only fathoms the numbers and since they are out of whack, he pulls out his trusty ax and slashes until something workable appears . . . projections that are incrementally higher, reached by doing last year harder!

So where does that leave us? At the very place where we should have begun our efforts in the first place . . . the strategies. Strategies drive all of the other components! Strategies help you run the business differently. Strategies address new markets and products or new operational efficiencies. They take more than one year to complete and are often cross-functional. Once you have developed and selected the array of strategies you plan to use to run the business differently, they will suggest how far you can go in what time and with what resources. You will find that the team will set more aggressive yet realistic goals and objectives when they know how they are going to get there. Once you have created the strategies and set the goals and objectives, it is easier to pull out all of the essentials for a good mission statement that is short and accurate with a sense of purpose.

Last but not least, you put legs under the strategy plan by developing all of the supporting tactics for each of the strategies. Strategies with their tactics will tell you what you need in resources to carry them out.

We do end up with the numbers after all. It is just that we arrive at them at the appropriate time—after the strategies are created, not before!

Chapter 15

Not All Strategies Are Created Equal

O nce you have created a wonderful array of new strategies, there is still work to be done on them. You must prioritize them for the company, or employees and managers will self select the ones that mean the most to them in their own areas and work on those first, even though these may not be the most critical ones for the organization as a whole. To avoid this "select from the menu" approach, the strategy team needs to take the time to prioritize the goals and strategies.

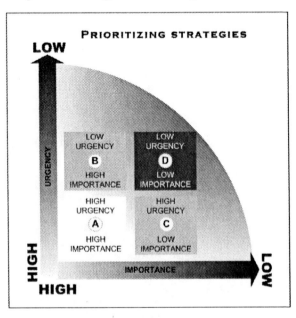

One easy way is to assign them a letter value according to importance or impact, usually dollars of profit, and urgency. A highly urgent and important strategy gets an A . . . that is a no brainer. But what is a B? Unfortunately, we are so trained to be very reactive to the current situation that we automatically move to what is urgent but not important . . . which is box C! Strategies that are important but not urgent are the foundation for your new future and cannot be pushed aside by a C. This is a common flaw of setting priorities.

Prioritizing Strategies

Use A, B, C, and D code letters to prioritize strategies as shown in the chart above.

The other aberration is to assign too many strategies an A priority. To emphasize everything is to emphasize nothing! I have seen clients push to have so many A's that they start to make categories within, such as A1, A2, and so on. You have four letters to work with and they should be distributed somewhat equally among your strategies. Then I hit them with the kicker! All of those strategies with a D . . . the D stands for "do not do"! This is one way to avoid wasting time on low-impact matters and free up time to work on high-impact matters.

Once priority letters are assigned, you can look over all the strategies assigned to each member of the team to make sure they are not overloaded, especially with A-level strategies. Also, do not stack all of the A strategies too early in the first year. Remember you still have a business to run, so do not let your excitement and optimism get the best of you. Spread all of the strategies out early on or you will have to make a lot of adjustments later.

Sometimes it is easier to think of strategies and their related goals as either primary ones or enablers. Primary ones are those that will generate improved profit dollars quickly, less than one year (an A priority). Some examples are reducing costs or increasing sales or margins by changing focus on customers or markets or products and product lines. Enablers are those strategies that help build the infrastructure for future growth. It takes longer to execute them and for them to pay off (two to three years) but they are essential in the long run. An example would be a new IT system. It may take a year to evaluate needs and select a system, another year to implement (if everything goes very, very, very well), with the payback starting in year three. Adding new plant, creating a new product line, and expanding internationally are other examples of enabling strategies.

You never want to front load (from a time standpoint) the plan with enablers. They cost real money with a slow payback and may stress your profits and cash flow early on. If your business is one of several in a larger corporation, such front loading may lead to the plan not being approved or funded. I suggest the bootstrap approach. Front load enough primary strategies so that they, in effect, pay for the enablers. A pay-as-you-go method will not require new outlays in order to execute the plan. It is a financially prudent way to proceed whether you have access to a lot of money or not.

Once in a while, if using letter categories is too difficult or not precise enough for your organization, you may want to go to the effort to ordinarily rank them. Again, there is the tendency to want to make several strategies number 1 . . . Resist! There is only one number 1, one number 2 and so on. The forced-ranking method may help, as shown below.

Never Waste Time on Low-Impact Matters

FORCED RANKINGS EXAMPLE

#1 = Most Important #5= Least Important						
Note: The lowest score is the top priority.						
	PERSON A RANKING	*PERSON B RANKING*	*PERSON C RANKING*	*PERSON D RANKING*	*PERSON E RANKING*	*TOTAL SCORE*	*GROUP RANK*
ISSUE A	2	4	1	1	4	12	2
ISSUE B	1	2	5	2	3	13	3
ISSUE C	4	5	2	5	2	18	4
ISSUE D	5	3	4	4	5	21	5
ISSUE E	3	1	3	3	1	11	1

Each team member individually ranks the strategies anonymously and then passes the sheet listing each of the strategies forward to be summarized on a flip chart. As long as the president does not do something unique to his/her sheet, all responses are seen as equal. Then it is a simple matter of arithmetic to sum the numbers for all of the strategies. The one with the lowest score is the highest priority. It is very easy to see the priorities at the top and the bottom.

Although the responses are semi-confidential, those who ranked an issue at either end of the range shown often speak up and indicate why they did so. This is another opportunity to examine underlying assumptions and values. You may take such "votes" several times before you end up with the final ranking. This process will get you there quickly while surfacing all of the pertinent issues. The important thing is that you somehow end up with priorities that individuals and the organization will follow.

Question: What major initiatives do you have underway currently? Are you making significant progress on them? Is it too many to be effective?

Notes:

Chapter 16

Rome Wasn't Built in a Day

A strategy plan certainly can and should have an immediate and positive impact, but most of it may take years to unfold. It is vital that realistic expectations be set in place for the different strategies, especially the enablers. Anything significant often takes a while to accomplish as shown below. It can take a significant amount of time, effort, and money before a strategy pays off. It is often eighteen months or more before an initiative's results exceed its investment; this is especially true for enablers. Employees, management, and especially the financial folks need to be periodically reminded that we are in it for the long haul and investing in the business. A preoccupation with quarterly results makes businesses far too impatient for results.

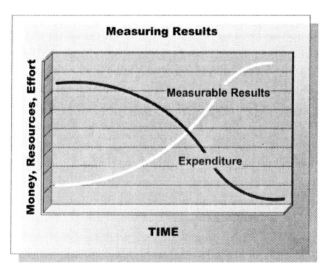

If businessmen were farmers, we all would be starving! At the end of the growing season, a farmer clears the land. In the spring, they spread herbicide and fertilizer, plow the field, seed and water and *wait* until the Fourth of July to see if the corn is knee high. The businessman would do all of the same steps through seeding and wait for a week, then dig it up to see why it wasn't sprouting yet! Anyone who has gone through a Total Quality Management (TQM) or process re-engineering project knows it takes time for some strategies to grab hold. Too often, if the current financials start to look rough, the folks in finance spot the initial expenditures and offer the strategy up to budget cutting at the most inopportune time after the big investment has been made and just prior to the payoff!

Naturally, you want to stay on target. Track to make sure expenses are not heading north and results south. If they do, take corrective action. But stick to the basic plan and strategy. Even when things are chugging along well, people can tire from the effort. Celebrate the small successes along the way and continue to communicate the long-term results that are coming down the pike.

Chapter 17

Now What?

If you have followed a process of the five D's, you may feel that you are done with your planning effort. You would be wrong. A few items need to be considered before proclaiming a plan complete.

Executives are sometimes startled to find that when the plan is released, it is met with thunderous nonapplause by the rest of the organization. This reaction should come as no surprise since creating all of the new exciting strategies is only half of a good process. You are laying significant new initiatives on an already overworked group of folks . . . no wonder they are not too excited. *When you add net new strategies, you also must clear away lower impact efforts or activities to allow time and resources to implement the new.* This reallocation of resources should be considered during every step of the five D's. If you do not, the plan will last a very long time because you will never get it done.

Clearing the plate not only invigorates the organization but it allows the new initiatives to proceed without adding a lot of additional cost. You will be reallocating resources from low—or no-impact activities to those with a higher, long-term impact. Unfortunately, this is a lot easier said than done. We cling to the old ways very strongly for a number of reasons. We may like doing them. We may be very good at them. We may have been well rewarded for them in the past and they may have helped us reach our current level of success. If we do not eliminate them, we will gravitate back to them. They will become resource suckers from the new initiatives.

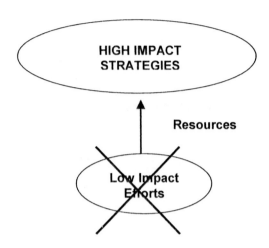

Now that we have the plan and have cleared away low-impact items, are we done? No. *Never create a new strategy without creating an exit strategy!* I do not mean to sound negative but there is not a new company, a new product or service, new location or new program that planned to fail! But they often do. The more innovative the strategy, the more risk it entails. Yes, we try to limit the risk with good research, and test programs but there still is and ought to be some risk. If you want to make inordinate profits, you must take inordinate risks. Try to contain the risk but also be ready to fix the strategy quickly or kill it if necessary. This contingency planning is as critical to your long-term success as the creation of strategy. Too many organizations have been seriously or fatally wounded by not being able to deal effectively with a strategy that just does not pan out.

It is easy to fall in love with our own ideas. Think of all the pet projects that are still hanging on to some sort of life in your organization that should have been killed years ago. They are often the sacred cows or taboos. Talking about the walking dead, some organizations feel more like a morgue than a hot bed of exciting new approaches. If you set up the appropriate measurements for success or failure ahead of time along with the actions to be taken when they are reached, it enables the organization to take quick remedial action when required. If you don't do this, when things head south, you will get caught in a series of endless meetings trying to define just how bad is bad while resources are frittered away on a doomed initiative.

For example, if a new product is planned to sell ten thousand units a month in the first six months, then what does nine thousand or eight thousand or seven thousand units mean? If you state that ten thousand is the plan, and seven thousand five hundred to eight thousand five hundred means it's time to rework the approach, and less than seven thousand, you kill it, then your course is clear. You do everything to make it happen and then let the chips fall where they may. Even in this example, there is a poor mental model at work. Failure is defined as too little success, but it can also come in the form of too much success. If ten thousand is the plan, then is twelve thousand better? How about fifteen thousand or eighteen thousand? If the product becomes a runaway, can you meet the customers' demand or will you disappoint them? Can you maintain the quality? Can you hit your target profitability when you have to work overtime and find additional materials on an emergency basis? It is far better to use a range that covers both ends of the spectrum of failure—too little and too much of a good thing.

Now you must be thinking, we are finally done, we have the plan, we have exit strategies and we have cleared the decks of the organization for implementation. Unfortunately, you are not quite done. Your organization is stuck in a habit pattern of doing exactly what it does now—running as is. This habit pattern is very difficult to break; it may have been going on for years. It will not change on its own no matter how good your intentions. You will have to put in some structures to force the organization out of its old habits so it can pursue the new strategies you have developed. I call this process "Changing the Gates."

Chapter 18

Changing the Gates

Experienced farmers will tell you how to lead hogs happily to the slaughter line just by setting up a series of gates in the holding pen. The hogs will naturally and voluntarily, yet unintentionally, move toward the slaughterhouse. Now, I am not implying that having your employees follow your new strategy plan is like going to slaughter, though some may act like it is, but to point out that they will need some serious nudging to find the new path. It is only natural that people will gravitate back to their old ways no matter how compelling a new plan may be. The following gates will help employees in the organization move forward whether they want to or not!

Change Peoples' Behavior Or Change The People

Your new strategies are not voluntary. They are not menu items from which your employees can choose the portions they like. *Your strategies are mandatory.* Commitment to the plan is essential to its execution and this is especially true for top management. Failure to comply for any reason must be subject to severe consequences, at a minimum, reassignment to a non-strategic area or reassignment outside of the organization! Execution of a plan is like entering battle . . . deserters are shot and conscientious objectors are re-assigned to alternate duty. In either case, they are replaced by those who can and will carry out the battle plan.

This may sound like a harsh approach, but lack of commitment is probably the number one reason that new plans are poorly carried out, creating a corresponding lack of meaningful results. If a top manager does not support the effort wholeheartedly, you lose the efforts of all who report to this individual. A manager cannot allow those he leads not to follow the plan. If such wavering occurs at any level, it is like a cancer that will spread to the rest of the organization and send a signal that the plan is optional. One way to avoid such a situation is to involve as many people throughout the planning process as possible. Make sure they understand the reasoning behind the plan, its strategic intent. We will discuss this further in the chapters on developing an effective planning process.

Change The Reward System If You Want Employees To Pursue New Strategies

Managers and employees alike are very adept at figuring out how to maximize their own income and will follow whatever actions will help them do so. Most reward systems are set up to encourage the current business strategies and must be realigned to the new set of strategies. A realignment of rewards involves a focus on new strategies and goes beyond one year if you are to succeed in creating significant change. Anything of significant impact will take longer than one year to fully implement.

Change Some Of Your Basic Processes

Your current processes support your current strategies. New strategies require new processes so they will be carried out effectively. This is the area where most business books and consultants live. Such efforts include what is hot and what is not in the business community, including process re-engineering, TQM, Six Sigma, reduced cycle times, Theory of Constraints, and the list goes on and on. Do not get me wrong; I am not knocking these approaches. They can be very useful in and of themselves, but they are the most effective when they are in service of clearly thought through and articulated strategies. They are the tactics of the strategy plan and are used in combination with others to implement the strategies. They also create a method in which to lead employees to change their behavior, which is so crucial to success.

Change The Organization Structure

New strategies often require new roles, changed roles, and new positions in your organization. Such restructuring of roles and positions helps codify the changes in behavior that are expected to occur and give individuals clear cut responsibilities and accountabilities to achieve them. For example, bricks and mortar retailers had to create new positions, and sometimes, a new organization structure in order to tap into the opportunities and challenges offered by e-commerce. Developing a totally new strategy may require skill sets that do not exist in the organization. It may not be possible or timely to try to develop the capability internally, thus creating a key situation where an organizational change is required.

Change The Way You Communicate Your Strategies To The Organization

Most strategy plans are introduced to the organization with a big bang, and the excitement fizzles quickly for a variety of reasons.

Communications experts say that you must follow the seven-by-seven rule if you want to reach people. In essence, you need to communicate to them at least seven times and seven different ways before a concept actually sets in. Very different from the one-time shot so often used. Different people respond to different communication approaches. Some respond to the verbal message, others to the written, some like to see graphs and charts or a combination of all of the above. It may seem unnecessary, yet, it is critical. Why do you think the United Way uses the thermometer to post its progress towards its fund-raising goals? The answer is: Because it is so effective in communicating progress! Why do credit card companies keep sending out those solicitation letters and calls to the effect of twenty per year for every person in the U.S.A.? (Over five billion a year!) They know it takes many different contacts before an impression (sale) occurs. There is a lot of science behind this concept that marketers use. Organizations need to market new strategies to their internal customers . . . their employees.

Repeat the essence of your strategies in newsletters, employee meetings, e-mails, videos, employee reviews, employee training . . . whenever and wherever you can.

An easy and powerful method to reinforce the new plan with employees is on a one-to-one basis. Every time you ask an employee to change their behavior or do something new, you should quickly tie the request back to one or more of the new strategies in the plan. It makes it very real for them and helps to offset the natural tendency to resist change. *We often spend so much time telling employees what to do that we fail to tell them the strategic intent or the why of it.* No job is so structured that an employee does not have to make any decisions. If the employee knows the intent behind your strategies, he or she can make those decisions so that they will support the plan rather than unintentionally thwart the spirit of the plan.

Chapter 19

No Stealth Plans

You will want to develop a formal communication plan for the new strategy plan. If communication of the plan is left up to the top executives to carry out, it will end up looking like you have as many plans as you do top executives! They are not all created equal and will have varying abilities and styles of communication. They will be influenced by their functional position as to what is important in the plan and what is not. They may even decide how much of the plan should be communicated. A structured communication methodology will go a long way towards eliminating such variations and ensure a consistent rollout of the strategies throughout the organization. The communication plan should include what should be covered at each level of the organization, who should cover it, when it should be covered, and how it should be consistently re-communicated and in what ways.

Often, companies end up having a stealth plan—we have it but you cannot see it. While teaching strategy development in the Executive MBA program at the University of St. Thomas in the Twin Cities, I am often reminded of how poorly strategy plans are communicated. These seasoned managers, with an average age of forty-two years and ten years management experience, nearly have to sign in blood to see a copy of their company's strategy plan for comparison to some of the concepts used in the text. How can they help carry out a plan they have not even seen? Worse yet, this is not just an oversight but intentional! Top management indicates it is confidential. After all, they would not want the competition to get their hands on it!

What is worse—your competition seeing a plan that uniquely matches your company's abilities or having your own employees ignorant of it with no real chance to help implement it more effectively? After all, seeing it doesn't mean competitors can implement it or block it. A sharp competitor can eventually figure out your plan by watching your behavior, so why insult your employees by not trusting them with the information. You do not need to share all of the precise numbers and nitty-gritty details, just the basic mission, goals and key strategies.

The list below covers the basics of communicating a plan well. It is essential that you not only communicate the plan but the underlying strategic intent and the rationale behind the strategies. If your people understand the strategic intent, then they can carry out their related actions more effectively and in line with the new strategies. No plan can or should be so detailed that an individual does not have some discretion in how they undertake their jobs. They will always have to make choices day in and day out how to best implement the strategies. They may do something that from their perspective makes great sense but, in effect, is the opposite of the intent of the strategy. As a result, you can never spend too much time on explaining and clarifying the strategic intent.

Unfortunately, as the communication triangle below demonstrates, most organizations spend too much time on task talk (what we want you to do) in their daily communications and not enough on the strategic talk (why we want you to do it). Let me share an exercise that I use with executives to drive home the importance of this point. Follow these instructions.

1. On the top half of a clean sheet of paper, draw a triangle.
2. Now connect a straight line to the triangle.
3. Underneath all of that, draw a banana.
4. Underneath all of that, draw a series of lower case script w's.

You have been subjected to nothing but task talk. Did you end up with a sailboat? Probably not, but I gave you specific instructions for the sail (triangle), the mast (straight line), the boat (banana), and the water (the w's). Now if I had said at the beginning we are going to draw a sailboat (the strategic intent), then the outcome would have been different! This exercise usually gets everyone chuckling a bit. The sad thing is that each of us spends too much time each day on task talk and not enough on quality talk or strategic intent!

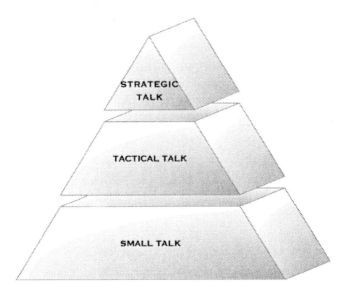

Question: What are some methods you can use to communicate and reinforce strategies to those involved in implementing them?

Notes:

Chapter 20

The Four C's of a Well-Written Plan

A good strategy plan must be well documented. A verbal strategy plan is not worth the paper it is written on! However, do not get carried away. You do not want a three-inch binder that weighs ten pounds and collects dust on the top shelf because nobody looks at it or uses it until the next planning cycle begins! (I know some readers are cringing right about now.) The following four C's should help you avoid this all-too-common malady.

Comprehensive

The plan should be comprehensive. It should cover all of the new strategies, any mission revisions, a brief executive overview, and possibly a little bit of tactical detail for flavor. This is the easy C!

Concise

The plan should be concise! It is a summary document, brief, and to the point. It is in outline form with key points and bullets. Remember the Ten Commandments . . . the Bible provides further details. The strategy plan is analogous to the Ten Commandments and the Bible to the details of the annual tactical plan. A concise strategy plan is short and full of impact, often no more than several pages.

I know many of you think this is impractical and would like

a more recent example than one from biblical times. Below is a seven-line strategy plan that guided the largest organization of people on earth at the time.

It was the early 1940s and the organization was the Allied forces in World War II. It was developed by Churchill, Stalin, and Roosevelt, certainly a true cross-functional team of diverse personalities and perspectives, if there ever was one.

**Unconditional Surrender
(The Goal)**

The Strategies

**IN WAR—RESOLUTION
IN DEFEAT—DEFIANCE
IN VICTORY—MAGNANIMITY
IN PEACE—GOODWILL**

TWO-FRONT WAR—GERMANY FIRST

Short, comprehensive and full of impact . . . the plan for winning World War II. Sure, there were many specific battle plans that were to follow but the basic plan outlined above was carried out. In defeat—defiance led to the French underground resistance. In victory—magnanimity and in peace—goodwill led to the Marshall Plan.

The Marshall Plan was the most significant investment in resources on a global basis ever to rebuild the economies and infrastructure of former enemies. In addition, the requirement of unconditional surrender led to the unleashing of the most destructive force known to mankind—the dropping of the atomic bomb on Hiroshima and Nagasaki. Impactful indeed!

The following chart is an example of a simple project plan document we use with clients. Ten to twelve pages can turn a large organization inside out, upside down, and sideways. The pages should get dog eared and marked up—in other words, it should get used and reviewed.

STRATEGY DEVELOPMENT PLAN FORMAT						
GOAL:						
OBJECTIVE:						
Priority	Strategy	Actions Tactics	Champion	Time Frame	Resources Required	Expected $ Outcomes

Clear

The plan should be clear to the layperson. So many plans are laden with internal jargon and acronyms, you need a translation code to decipher the true meaning. It should make sense to any new employee or outsider who reads it.

Communicated

The plan can and should be shared beyond the organization as well as within. Key customers and vendors may be interested in knowing where you are headed and what it will mean to them in the future. Can you meet their developing needs? Will you require different resources from vendors and suppliers? Do not forget strategic partners. For example, personal-computer manufacturers share their new product plans with software companies so that application software will be developed at the same time the product is, which makes the most use of its new capabilities. Consumer-product makers that sell through retailers must communicate their desires to the stores for more or different shelf space as much as two years in advance. Bankers need to understand what type of financial resources you will require to implement the new strategies. Do not forget to communicate with these external resources.

Chapter 21

Warming Up to Change

People react to large changes in many different ways at different times. The organization needs some time to assimilate the new strategies and their impact on each individual. Despite all of the literature suggesting that change is life, and that it is constantly surrounding and involving all of us, I believe that most people are reluctant to change unless absolutely necessary. We all have habits that are not only comfortable but have worked well for us in the past. We may not want to give these up for the sake of corporate improvement.

During the data-collection phase of our strategy development process, we identified all of the reasons for change. These reasons need to be communicated during quality talk with all employees. It is easier to accept change when it is driven by the external world, such as competitors, or customers, or technology, and our future is dependent upon making the changes. It is not because we have not been doing a good job or working hard or just change for change's sake to use the latest technique of the month. It is required to move forward. Not moving forward in a time of change is to move backwards with all of its consequences.

Passivity is not a strategy. The old adages that "ignorance is bliss" and "good things come to those who wait" implies that if you are dumb enough, long enough, you will be just fine. Though passivity is a common default strategy, it does not work. Remember as W.C. Fields once said "Even a dead fish can make its way down stream." There are really only two types of challenges that confront an organization . . . growth challenges and liquidation challenges. Growth challenges are better!

Employees need time to process the coming change and grieve for the old ways. The change process is like the grieving process when one loses a loved one. Many of the steps are the same.

1. Denial: It will not really happen! They will never do it. I will just wait until this too passes over.
2. Bargaining: We will get you the revenue or cost reductions you want; just do not change our ways. We will do last year harder!
3. Anger: You really are going to make the changes you (explicative of your choice)! Well, I do not have to like or support it other than lip service.
4. Fear: What does this all mean to me and what I do and how I do it? Can I be successful at it?
5. Confusion: What do I do now?
6. Acceptance: I will do the best I can under the circumstances?
7. Moving on: It wasn't so bad after all . . . I wonder what's next?

People go through these stages at different speeds and linger at certain stages longer than others. The key point is that people progress through the steps, and laggards are not left too far behind. The tough part is that everyone must get to the stage of acceptance in a reasonable length of time. If they cannot, then they need to find another organization that is better suited to them. You cannot let a select few hold back the organization or undertake passive resistance.

Moreover, this is not just applicable to the lower and middle levels of the organization but to the very top as well. Solid followership is essential at the top! If a department head does not follow the strategy, you lose the effort of the entire organization below.

Chapter 22

Leading a Strategy Session

F riends, colleagues, and potential clients often ask me what our strategy development meetings are like. It is difficult to describe for a number of reasons. First, most folks do not grasp how much preparation is done before the first meeting, including all of the data collection and analysis. This preparation actually allows the meetings to become very creative and free-flowing. There are no slowdowns due to lacking information or analysis. Also, the advance analysis unveils potential strategies that the participants are eager to get out on the table.

Discussion Flow

In theater, a director tells all of the actors what he wants to accomplish. In a mob scene featuring hundreds of actors, it is impossible to tell each individual actor where to stand, walk, and talk. It is well crafted and planned chaos, letting the actors do their own thing once they have been prepped. This is very similar to a good strategy session. Once it starts rolling, you never quite know exactly where you will end up, but I can assure you, it will be far different from where you are now.

The data collection assignments are loosely used as agenda items for the sessions. I usually start with the front-wheel subjects (customer profile and products and services analysis) first. Discussions on these topics naturally flow to other assignments. There are no hard and fast rules about the order they are covered in the meeting.

Everyone asks the order so they may wait until the last minute before completing the assignment! All the assignments must be completed before the first session. If everyone is well prepared, they can jump into a discussion to agree, disagree, or amplify a point based on their discoveries during their assignments. This approach really gets the energy flowing.

It is natural to have some heated debates and that is not only OK, it is what you want. Passionate debate shows what people really feel and perceive based on their assumptions and values. It is essential to bring these feelings out and deal with them. Do not discourage such arguments for the sake of decorum but let them roll along with the creative output that gushes forth. I just draw the line at physical violence, especially if it is directed at the outside consultant!

Passion is great; a lack of passion is the kiss of death to creativity and innovation. When things get a little too heated, you can throw in a bit of humor to defuse it or take a break so people can calm down and refocus on the task at hand. It is far easier to crank back an excited group than it is to try to pump up a group that is listless.

Role of the CEO

The CEO needs to be prepared for a different role in the meeting than he is accustomed to playing. Rather than lead the discussion, the CEO needs to lay back and listen. This approach forces the team to put their thoughts on the table without the CEO guiding the discussion. He may be surprised by what he hears. Many managers are very astute at assessing which way the leader is leaning and either consciously or unconsciously move to that position. This is to be avoided at all costs. Having the CEO hold off on his points until all the others are made will help loosen up the discussion.

In the meetings, the leader can really see what his people think and what they are capable of doing. He can see which ones are strategic and which are not. Team players stand out. Some participants will blossom and others will not. The meetings often present him with a new perspective of his team. He does not relinquish his control since he does get to get his thoughts in at the end of a discussion. However, I have often observed that the CEO is the one who changes his perceptions the most once he sees what strategies his team really has a passion to pursue. What the team comes up with may not exactly match up to the CEO's views but they will implement their strategies far better if they are their own and not just the CEO's.

Time for Meetings

One caveat to follow is to keep meetings short. I have done the traditional two eight-hour days back to back. I learned that you can get a group to agree to anything on the last half of the second day. If you meet for eight hours, you get about five to six hours of true strategizing because the team runs out of gas.

Four-hour meetings work great for strategy development. Participants are fresh and can stay with the meeting. Phone breaks are minimized since they have half the day to still take care of business. Also, shorter, more frequent meetings help avoid the stupid days. Yes, I said stupid days! Everyone has them from time to time and so do groups. It may be that they are distracted by a recent crisis or are tired or it's the best weather of the month! A stupid half-day is better than two stupid full days.

Taking Notes

Lastly, be sure to have a noncombatant, excuse me, a nonparticipant take thorough notes throughout the meeting. This system allows everyone to listen closely to the discussion that is taking place since they will not be distracted by taking notes. Never, never, never let one of the managers involved in the session take the notes. I have a saying about meeting notes—he who takes the notes wins! It is only natural that the notes will subtly reflect the taker's perceptions. And don't kid yourself by rotating the note taker for each session, it will still show biases and take a key player out of the discussion.

It is a simple concept to have objective notes taken each session, but one that is often neglected. The notes should include:

- Additional data needed and who is to collect it
- The potential strategies developed
- Data the assumptions are based upon
- Decisions made

Poor note taking leads to differences of opinion by team members after the fact. It is critical that the notes are adjusted if necessary and agreed to at the onset of each successive meeting. The strategy plan is drawn from the notes, so it is important they are accurate. The agreement to the notes forces people to review them and builds consensus and commitment as you go forward. It is important to get them out the day after the meeting so they can be digested well before the next meeting

A cautionary point is in order. Note taking for strategy development meetings is not a court-reporter function. You do not need to know exactly what every person said, just the gist of the discussion as noted above. Attribution of statements will throw cold water on creative discussion. It is an important job and must be assigned to a very capable and objective person. This person is as critical as any member of the strategy development team!

Do not let waiting for the presentation of the final plan become a straight jacket to implementation. It is both normal and expected that after a particularly rousing and effective session, the team may want to start implementing a new strategy right away. That is just great as long as they have had some time to sleep on it to be sure it is what they truly want to do. Usually after such a meeting and a review of the notes, one of three things occurs:

1. They want to start immediately.
2. They have some new data or perspectives that have arisen through their discussion with others not on the team.

3.   They wonder what they were smoking that day when they came up with a particular strategy . . . the reason you give it some time to be chewed upon!

Remember, undocumented potential strategies are not worth the paper they are written on!

Chapter 23

Monitoring the Plan

The primary responsibility for monitoring the strategy plan falls to those team members assigned a particular strategy. They become the strategy champions. It is essential that this responsibility fall to one person, not a committee. The effort can get lost in the shuffle of a team and an individual is more committed to its completion than a whole team. You want to be able to hold a person accountable . . . rewarding him or her for excellence and applying corrective action when needed.

The strategy development team provides the next level of accountability. The team should periodically review the progress of the strategies. This review occurs monthly for larger organizations, and quarterly for smaller ones. If you have never implemented a strategy plan or not done it well, then you should monitor it monthly no matter what your size.

Monitoring the plan need not take a lot of time. I suggest using a stand-up meeting for the review. You only need to assess the status of each initiative, not listen to long narratives on how well things are going. A stand-up meeting will keep it brief, especially if it is scheduled for the end of the day! I prefer that everyone use the stoplight method of status reporting. If the strategy is on track, it is labeled green so you can quickly move on. If it is labeled yellow, it needs some attention and if it is labeled red, it needs a whole lot of attention.

Do not try solving the yellow and red strategies at the meeting; it will waste the time of those not involved. Set up side meetings for those who are impacted. Never schedule your strategic reviews at the end of the monthly operating review meeting. These are completely different types of meetings—one very short-term oriented and the other one longer term. Too often, the strategic review is hastily done or not done at all because time is short. Set up the review meeting dates in advance on the calendar for the coming year so they will not be missed.

The sheer fact of holding monthly review meetings will help ensure implementation progress. I assure you, no one will want to come to more than one or two meetings in a row with their strategies classified as yellow or red. Also there are lots of great project management programs available that can be used by the strategy development team to keep everyone up to date. A sample of the simple format we use is below:

STRATEGY DEVELOPMENT PLAN FORMAT						
GOAL: OBJECTIVE:						
Priority	Strategy	Actions Tactics	Champion	Time Frame	Resources Required	Expected $ Outcomes

The reviews let you take a look at the overall plan. It is important to make any necessary adjustments in tactics, and maybe even a strategy, if the external world changes more than assumed in the plan.

Remember, you do not ring the cash register until the plan is implemented!

Chapter 24

The Plan as a Roadmap

Once you have developed and prioritized all of the new strategies, you have the basics of the roadmap to your new future. But having the right direction does you no good if you just sit in the middle of the road! You have to begin the journey.

There are a couple of guidelines to bear in mind as you lock on to the measurements you will be using to check your progress, using the tactical one-year operating plan portion of the strategy plan. As discussed earlier, objectives are measurable and dated, not only for the annual portion, but also for the length of the planning horizon you utilized. When setting objectives, use a number range, make sure the objectives reward the right behavior, and set completion dates for the objectives.

It is very common to use a hard and fast number for an objective. For example, an objective may be for your sales to move from $100 million to $110 million for the first year with a corresponding improvement in profit from $5 million to $6 million. Utilizing number ranges for objectives is more realistic, more motivational, and less destructive than pinpoint objectives. This range does not lessen the focus on the objective . . . you still need to put the arrow somewhere on the target!

The problem with pinpoint numbers is that they imply that we can forecast with some degree of accuracy and we know that is not the case. Using such precise numbers can have some pretty negative effects on your efforts to execute your strategies.

If compensation is tied to reaching the numbers (which it should be) then hard numbers can lead to some very counterproductive behaviors relative to the long term. We have seen many public cases where managers have slanted, fudged or outright distorted the numbers to meet the objectives. This can involve misstating sales, shipments, and expenses or stuffing the distribution channel. Or, if it looks like the objective numbers have been made, there may be efforts to move additional business back to the next year or pull expenses forward to bank some extra profit for the coming year. Yes, some of these activities have been happening for years but it is too easy for it to get out of hand, especially when you are trying to meet an objective number that is a guesstimate at best.

Another issue is the motivation of your employees. If $110 million is success, then does that mean that $109 million is failure even though it is a healthy 9 percent more than last year? Any archer or dart player knows that a target is made up of ranges. You do not have to hit only a bull's eye to score or win. You can win a baseball game more often with bunts, singles and doubles than always swinging for the fence. The same applies to objectives. Objectives are not only measurable but also dated. I have looked far and wide and have yet to find ASAP (As Soon As Possible) on any calendar! But I do find a lot of ASAP's on the initial draft of objectives. This is not a measurement but a hope. Date the objectives so you can effectively track progress. Be realistic, you still have a business to run as you implement change.

Now, let me throw in a ringer or two to the above rule on dates. First, some changes may occur immediately and become ongoing; and it is perfectly alright to note them this way. Secondly, there may be occasions where an event, rather than a hard date, is more useful and effective. For example, based upon your sales forecast (think guesstimate), you plan to break ground on a new plant or distribution center in the second quarter of the second year. The strategy is in the approved capital budget. What happens if sales are lower than expected? Since it is in the budget and approved, the project often proceeds. What if sales are way ahead of schedule? Do you stick with the date?

Why not consider triggering a strategy by an event rather than a date? For the above example, the ground breaking would occur when sales have achieved a specified level or rate. This approach allows for automatic adjustment of the next strategy, either forward or backward in time. It helps build in flexibility to the strategies, just as do ranges for the objectives . . . the strategy plan is a directional roadmap. It should not be a straight jacket . . . there will be detours along the way!

Chapter 25

Do It Right or Not at All

As I stated earlier, creative strategy development is neither rocket science nor terribly difficult, but it does take time and effort. That is the reason it is so often delayed or avoided. It is so much easier to just go for incremental improvements to the current operations (staying on the first curve). It provides immediate, although smaller gains and gratification. However, significant improvement requires significant effort.

The approach I have outlined in this book is not a difficult one to follow. It is general enough and with slight modifications can be adapted to any organization's situation. It has room to include any of your favorite tools and methodologies. Remember the process that you use, or don't use, will have a great impact on the strategies you develop.

Strategy development is the time to use the KISS principle (Keep It Simple, Stupid). Do not go crazy or get wrapped around the axle by trying to do an elaborate plan, especially the first time. You may spend too much time on the process and end up with paralysis of analysis. **A good plan now is far more useful than a better plan later!**

What's Required

The strategy development team must make the following commitments to create successful strategy plans.

STRATEGY DEVELOPMENT COMMITMENTS REQUIRED	
Planning Becomes Management's Top Priority	Management needs to be willing to make this process their top priority, attend all "core group" meetings, and spend 40 to 60 hours or more over a three to four-month period on strategy development. This priority also needs to be extended beyond the project so that follow-up and implementation also become a priority.
The Sharing of Decision-Making is Endorsed	Top management needs to be willing to share decision-making with those affected by the decision. This specifically means that the CEO should be willing to share the decision-making among the groups set up for strategy development—the core group, the management group, and the input groups. There should also be a willingness to have each strategy development team member fill out a thorough questionnaire about how he or she feels about the organization's ability to effectively manage resources, people, tasks and processes. However, shared decision-making should not be used to avoid decision-making. Top management still needs to take the input and make the tough decisions—where are we going?
There is a Free Flow of Sensitive Information	The CEO should be willing to listen to and encourage the discussion of all information. Management must want to encourage mutual trust and open communication.
Develop a Climate Which Encourages and Rewards New Ideas, Irreverent Candor and Willingness to Change	Management must be willing to turn over every stone and objectively look at each option. There must be fertile ground for new ideas.
There is a High Investment in Maintaining Strategic Thinking	The commitment for strategic thinking needs to extend beyond the formal planning project. Management needs to be willing to set up regular follow-up sessions to check progress of implementation and re-evaluate and update the plan on a regular basis.
Rewards are Based on Achievement of the Objectives of the Plan	Management needs to be willing to restructure the formal and informal reward systems in the organization to tie in with the achievement of their mission and objectives.
Patience, Patience, Patience	Top management needs to realize that change is painful and slow. Good plans require time, thorough research and detailed analysis of the current situation. The tedious process of understanding where you are now and how you can develop into a better team will pay off in the long run.

What Are The Pitfalls To Avoid During The Process

Strategy development has its pitfalls, but these pitfalls can be overcome. Awareness of them is the key.

STRATEGY DEVELOPMENT PITFALLS TO AVOID	
Overplanning	The organization must be action oriented and willing to sacrifice detail in plans for an "act on" orientation.
Quick Fixes	Successful planning requires a commitment to the long-term. You need the discipline to regularly and consistently engage your organization in planning. It takes time, and you cannot evaluate the benefits solely by short-term results.
Not Digging Deep Enough or Stretching	An organization must be willing to explore areas which may not be easy or comfortable. There must be a high commitment to stretching, challenging and excelling.
Not Involving Key People	If a plan is to be accepted and implemented, it must be properly communicated and should regularly involve as many employees as possible.
Weak Follow-Up	Annual plans should be created and maintained via regular, consistently scheduled, fully attended follow-up meetings.
Unwilling to Change or Make Tough Decisions	Successful planning implies making tough decisions and eventual changes in the organization.
Poor Support From Top Management	Planning cannot be fully delegated—it requires full-time continued commitment in thought, words and deeds from top management.
Unwilling to Change	For a plan to work effectively, the structure of an organization must change to support and implement the strategy.
Lack of Teamwork or Organizational Development	Managers and employees must be willing to build a team and work together.

If you cannot do it right—don't do it! A half-baked attempt will not succeed and will harm your organization more than it helps. It will also make any future attempts much more difficult. Stay the course and your organization will be well rewarded with a much brighter future. But, also keep in mind, anything worth doing is worth doing imperfectly.

> Everyone thinks of changing the world but no one thinks of changing himself.
> —Tolstoy

Exhibit A

Questions cover all areas of the organization. Respondents rate their level of concern from 1-10 (10 being high). A zero response means they do not know and is not counted in the average.

For confidentiality, the raw scores are scrambled so no one column represents a person yet the raw scores are shown.

Average of the scores not counting zeros.

Percent of respondents who answered with a 1-10 score.

A, B, C representing highest averages.

BUSINESS SITUATION ANALYSIS SURVEY SAMPLE QUESTIONS	A	R	C	D	E	F	AVG	PRIORITY	RESPONSE %
PURPOSE OF COMPANY									
1. Company's mission is not clearly defined or understood	4	1	7	6	1	1	3.3		100%
2. Company's mission is out of date.	4	1	7	6	1	1	3.3		100%
3. Not clear where organization is headed.	3	2	6	2	1	2	2.7		100%
FORMAL ORGANIZATIONAL STRUCTURE									
1. Too many people report to one person.	3	1	5	2	1	3	2.5		100%
2. Personnel are not given sufficient direction.	7	1	3	2	2	5	3.3		100%
COMPANY LEADERSHIP									
1. Shoots from the hip too often.	6	2	4	2	1	2	2.8		100%
2. One person show.	5	1	3	1	1	5	2.7		100%
COMPANY PERSONNEL									
1. Standards of performance are not clear.	1	2	3	5	5	7	3.8		100%
2. Poor recruiting/selection.	1	4	1	1	2	4	2.2		100%
3. Reward system is inadequate.	1	4	2	1	1	2	1.8		100%
PLANNING									
1. Plans are not realistic.	5	1	8	4	4	2	4		100%
2. Plans are not clear or agreed on.	5	1	6	6	4	5	4.5		100%
3. Plans are not implemented.	7	1	7	6	9	5	5.8	B	100%
4. Resources are allocated by politics or who complains the most.	3	1	4	3	5	1	2.8		100%
CONTROL									
1. Too few rules/policies.	5	1	2	4	2	5	3.2		100%
2. No feedback on how we are doing.	5	1	4	3	2	5	3.3		100%
3. People are not held accountable.	7	1	3	5	8	8	5.3	B	100%
COORDINATION AND COMMUNICATION									
1. Sometimes we work against each other.	6	4	4	4	5	5	4.7		100%
2. Meetings unproductive.	6	1	3	5	9	5	4.8	C	100%
3. Poor work flow.	5	5	4	4	8	2	4.7		100%

CULTURE OF THE COMPANY								
1. Too much conflict.	5	3	3	4	7	3	4.2		100%
2. Too much dead wood (non productive/non contributing personnel).	2	1	7	2	5	1	3.		100%
3. We-they attitudes.	3	6	5	7	5	2	4.7		100%
4. Too much analysis, not enough action.	5	1	1	2	6	1	2.7		100%
MARKETING									
1. No market penetration plan.	8	3	5	3	1	2	3.7		100%
2. Slow to respond to market changes.	7	5	6	3	3	3	4.5		100%
3. Lack of or inadequate cross selling of products and services.	6	1	3	1	4	1	2.7		100%
4. Not sure what competition is doing.	7	3	6	7	4	6	5.5	B	100%
5. Don't know our customers.	5	1	5	4	1	2	3		100%
PRODUCTS/SERVICES									
1. Our products/services are outdated.	5	1	3	3	3	1	2.7		100%
2. Inadequate information developed on new products/services profitability.	7	4	4	4	8	6	5.5	B	100%
3. Poor products/services research data available in our industry.	0	3	5	5	2	1	3.2		83%
ACCOUNTING									
1. Poor cost analysis/information by:									
a. Department	4	8	5	7	1	0	5	C	83%
b. Product/product line	4	8	1	7	1	0	4.2	C	83%
c. Operating division	4	8	0	7	1	0	5	C	67%
FINANCIAL MANAGEMENT									
1. Unprofitable products/services are not clearly identified.	4	6	6	7	2	6	5.2	C	100%
2. Inadequate attention to delinquent accounts.	1	1	1	2	1	0	1.2		83%
DATA PROCESSING									
1. Too much information from computer.	1	2	2	1	1	2	1.5		100%
2. Poor software.	4	3	6	3	3	6	4.2		100%

							Avg.		%
OFFICE ADMINISTRATION									
1. Poor office procedures.	5	2	3	2	5	3	3.3		100%
2. Poor/inefficient work flow.	6	4	6	3	6	3	4.7		100%
3. Devote too much time to unnecessary tasks.	6	1	5	2	2	3	3.2		100%
PURCHASING									
1. Too many "rush" orders.	3	1	6	4	3	4	3.5		100%
2. Too many orders received late.	3	0	4	2	3	3	3		83%
3. Inadequate information available to facilitate purchasing decisions.	5	3	4	3	3	2	3.3		100%
4. Inefficient purchasing decisions.	5	1	4	2	3	6	3.5		100%
INVENTORY MANAGEMENT									
1. Inadequate information available to make inventory decisions.	7	0	0	4	8	6	6.3	A	67%
2. Too many stockouts.	5	0	2	2	7	2	4		67%
3. Low inventory turnover.	5	0	0	4	9	5	5.8	B	67%
4. Inadequate inventory planing.	5	0	0	3	6	2	4		67%
PRODUCTION									
1. Underutilization of manpower and equipment.	6	6	8	1	4	4	4.8	C	100%
2. Inadequate scheduling.	5	2	7	1	4	4	3.8		100%
3. Unrealistic shipping dates.	1	1	5	1	3	1	2		100%
4. Too many reworks.	9	10	8	6	8	8	8.2	A	100%
OUTPUT/RESULTS									
1. Too many projects fail.	2	3	6	1	3	8	3.8		100%
2. Mediocrity is accepted.	5	2	7	2	3	4	3.8		100%
3. Profitability is declining.	6	6	5	1	5	1	4		100%
4. Too much fire fighting.	5	2	5	6	6	5	4.8	C	100%
ENVIRONMENT									
On the next items, rate your level of concern over the possible adverse impact on the Company.									
1. Interest rates.	6	10	6	8	5	6	6.8	A	100%
2. Government regulation of the industry.	5	10	4	1	5	4	4.8	C	100%
3. Competitors.	5	10	2	5	4	7	5.5	B	100%

Priority Ratings and Average Scores in the range.

A = 8.2-6.2
B = 6.1-5.3
C = 4.8-6.0

The following pages represent samples of the write-in comments received on the questionnaires.

Please list below any additional concerns, problems or other topics.

- Change happens slowly.
- Documentation of product specs is weak. Sometimes we end up making the same product differently each times.
- More commitment to R&D is needed. Projects tend to drag out. This is due to our lack of adequate staffing and the "tyranny of the urgent."
- What happens if our product becomes outdated? We haven't given a lot of thought to what we would do.

What are the most critical issues which your company must face and resolve if it is to be successful in the future?

- Accountability.
- Be more aggressive in developing new products.
- Constantly being asked to produce a more difficult product with a less skilled work force.
- Find and keep good employees.
- Identify profitable products (current). Currently only look at bottom line and sguess what is profitable. Look at "losers" and delete or make profitable.

Please list the major strengths you see in your company. Be specific.

- A genuine concern for employees.

- A strong commitment to producing a quality product.
- Family owned.
- Financially stable.

How would your competitors describe your major weaknesses?
How would your customers describe your major weaknesses?

- Lack of empathy—"It's our way or the highway."
- Length of time to introduce new products.
- Our quality suffers when we become busy.
- Our turnaround time on quotes is too long.

Please list below major opportunities for growth, improved
profitability, improved customer service, etc., that you believe
should be considered by the company at this time.

- Concerted effort to major causes of rework and develop procedures to minimize it.
- Identify profit centers and expand.
- Improve customer service; turnaround time for quotes and acknowledgements.
- Improve lead time on R&D.

Please list the top external (outside our direct control) threats
facing the company.

- Tight labor market.
- Interest rates.
- Product supply.
- Aggressive new competitor.

Please describe the purpose of the company as you see it.

- Entrusted with a century-long reputation of integrity and excellence, we at are committed to ensuring the finest in quality, innovation, and efficient customer service. To accomplish this objective we will create and maintain a healthy work environment reinforced by team work between management and employees. In addition, we will promote a loyal network for quality product installation. The result of all our efforts is the total satisfaction of our customers, while preserving our natural resources and maintaining cutting-edge quality in the industry.

- To make money.